JOSEPH CONRAD
MASTER MARINER

Peter Villiers

JOSEPH CONRAD
MASTER MARINER

The novelist's life at sea, based on
a previously unpublished study by
ALAN VILLIERS

Illustrated with paintings of
vessels Joseph Conrad sailed in, by
MARK MYERS, RSMA, F/ASMA

SEAFARER BOOKS
SHERIDAN HOUSE

© Peter Villiers 2006

Published in the UK by
Seafarer Books · 102 Redwald Road · Rendlesham · Suffolk IP12 2TE · England
www.seafarerbooks.com
ISBN-10 0-9547062-9-3
ISBN-13 978-0-9547062-9-6

Published in the USA by
Sheridan House · 145 Palisade Street · Dobbs Ferry NY 10522 · USA
www.sheridanhouse.com
ISBN-10 1-57409-244-8
ISBN-13 978-1-57409-244-8

A CIP record for this book in the UK is available from the British Library
A CIP record for this book in the USA is available from the Library of Congress

Paintings © Mark Myers, RSMA, F/ASMA

Copy-editing: Hugh Brazier

Design and typesetting: Louis Mackay
Text set digitally in Proforma

Printed in China, on behalf of Compass Press Ltd,
via MBC Print Consultancy

Contents

Alan Villiers, 1903 –1982

Born in Melbourne, Australia, Alan Villiers went to sea aged 15 in the barque *Rothesay Bay* in the rough Tasman Sea. He sailed before the mast in the barques *James Craig*, *Bellands*, *Lawhill* and *Herzogin Cecilie*, and in the full-rigged ship *Grace Harwar*. From 1931, he was part-owner of the Finnish four-masted barque *Parma*, understudying her captain, the legendary Ruben de Cloux. In 1934 he sold his share in the *Parma* and purchased his own full-rigged ship, the Danish school-ship *Georg Stage*. He renamed her *Joseph Conrad* in honour of the great Polish sailor and writer, and sailed her round the world for two years. Determined to learn as much as he could about sail worldwide, he shipped in the Kuwaiti dhow *Triumph of Righteousness*, before World War II took him into the Royal Navy. Alan Villiers was renowned not only as a deep-water mariner, but also as a photographer and as the author of such classics of the sea as *The Set of the Sails*, *By Way of Cape Horn*, *Cruise of the Conrad*, *The Way of a Ship* and *Sons of Sindbad*.

Preface

My father, Alan Villiers, was a lifelong admirer of the works of the man whom he described as 'that brooding, Polish–English master mariner, Joseph Conrad'. Conrad's works had influenced him as a youth and young man, when he decided to go to sea for himself; and when he bought his own ship, the Danish *Georg Stage*, to sail around the world as a sail-training vessel, it was natural to rename her the *Joseph Conrad*. Under that name in 1934–36 she was to sail 57,800 miles around the world and to be at sea 555 days, until eventually sold in New York – a story told in the *Cruise of the Conrad*, now republished by Seafarer Books. The ship *Joseph Conrad* is now to be found, lovingly preserved, in the Mystic Seaport museum, Connecticut.

This, however, is the story of the seaman Joseph Conrad and not the ship named for him. Towards the end of a long, adventurous and astonishingly prolific life devoted to the love of ships and the sea, Alan Villiers decided to write a marine biography of Joseph Conrad. There was a mass of information available about Conrad as Pole, exile and writer. There were biographies and studies galore, and both British and American magazines, the *Conradian* and *Conradiana*, devoted to the study of most aspects of the great man's life and literature. However, there was rather less information and assessment available about Joseph Conrad as seafarer: and what there was did not tend, very naturally, to be written by experts in that area.

To the usual biographer, Conrad's sea-career was little more than a preamble, if a lengthy one, to his second and vastly more famous career as a writer. To Alan Villiers, a practical sailing-ship sailor and expert who had devoted his whole life to the sea, Conrad's merchant-navy career was of a unique interest in itself. Why did he first serve in the French merchant navy, and then the British? Why did he choose the ships in which he served, and what might he have learned from them? Was Conrad's merchant naval career orthodox or idiosyncratic? What was the merchant navy like in Conrad's time? It was not clear that such questions had ever been fully addressed, although many of the bare facts had been unearthed; and their answers might have much to reveal about Joseph Conrad.

Alan Villiers set out to research Joseph Conrad as seaman with his customary energy and determination, with his experience of sailing in the same waters and his perspective as a sailing-ship expert to guide him. He died in 1982 with his manuscript on Joseph Conrad incomplete: and so it remained until 2005, when I decided, perhaps with an inherited determination rather than a proper and fitting sense of my own inadequacy for the task, that so worthy an aim needed to be completed. My ambition was immediately and fully supported by the Conradian scholars whom I consulted, as well as by the host of people who remembered and cherished my father's work; and I was extremely fortunate to find a publisher with the vision to bring it to reality.

It has been an enduring challenge to have completed this work in the spirit in which my father would, I hope, have wished. I have not sought to imitate his inimitable style, or to assume his 'voice'. Those who know and love my father's writing will recognise his words where they emerge from the text in full and glorious flow, whether describing the passage of a ship under full sail, or offering some trenchant comment on the nature of life at sea. Some of my father's original material, therefore, remains in this text as he wrote it. I have added information which would not have been available to my father, where it serves to assist the purpose of the book; and I have needed to complete what he left unfinished and to edit what was unclear.

The result is, I hope, the essence of what my father, a professional sailor and appraiser of ships and shipping, made of Conrad as a long-term servant of ships and the sea. It has also been necessary to reflect on the state of the merchant navy in Conrad's day, so that his options and choices can be better evaluated; and here I have used both the notes left by my father for this manuscript and what he wrote elsewhere where relevant, including something on the evolution of sail into the twentieth century. Some of my father's opinions will, no doubt, be challenging, and I shall leave readers to find and decide what they may find controversial for themselves. Like my father, however, I have no doubt as to Conrad's essential greatness.

Sources on Conrad's merchant navy career in the late nineteenth century are varied. My father made use of first-hand sources where available, such as ships' logs, shipping records, and reports of courts of inquiry, and he made use of contemporary newspaper accounts where relevant. He considered and used Conrad's own account of his career under the red ensign, as published in various sources. There was also Conrad's correspondence, especially with his uncle and guardian, Tadeusz Bobrowski; and an increasing volume of biographical material, in which my father was especially interested in the discoveries made by Professor Norman Sherry in his two substantial volumes, *Conrad's Eastern World* and *Conrad's Western World*. To note one source, however, does not mean that others were neglected; and the resulting text is a synthesis of primary research and secondary commentary.

I have added only what seemed absolutely necessary in bringing my father's original research up to date, whilst retaining the flavour of his original work. Such references, old and new, accompany the text as footnotes. Short extracts from Conrad's own writings are taken from Dent's Collected Edition, particularly from *A Personal Record*, *The Mirror of the Sea*, *Notes on Life and Letters* and *Last Essays*.

These quasi-autobiographical musings are selective and must be handled with care. Conrad never intended them to be a full record of his life, and some commentators have pointed out errors in them. Moreover, whereas his fiction tends to treat the sea as it was, his memories and reflections offer a more romanticised view of the life of a sailor. Conrad did not take kindly to those who desired to delve into his past, especially if their intention were to verify the factual basis for his fiction. Like the veteran sailor Singleton of the *Narcissus*, we have therefore steered with care through these waters. It was never the intention of this book to offer yet another work on Conrad as writer, and where a correlation has been made between Conrad's merchant naval experience and the literature he produced later, this has been intended to assist the main purpose of the text and not as a gratuitous exercise in literary detection.

Acknowledgements

For his original research, enquiries and discoveries, Alan Villiers wished to acknowledge the help of Professor Edmund Bojarski of the University of Texas, then editor of *Conradiana*; Karl Kortum, director of the San Francisco Maritime Museum; Professor William Lyon Phelps of Yale University; Captain P. A. MacDonald, former master of the US four-masted barque *Moshulu*; Ronald Martin of the Public Records Office in Hayes, Middlesex, where many sailing-ship logs were stored; and two French former master mariners in sail, Marc Paillé of Nantes and Henri Picard of Royan. Many others helped my father in his inquiries, whose names have not been recorded: to those, also, we offer our thanks. They must include the staff, officials and supporters of the National Maritime Museum in Greenwich and the Society for Nautical Research, as well as other professional colleagues who assisted Alan Villiers in his quest.

The following have been of especial assistance in the completion of this manuscript in the twenty-first century. Patricia Eve, the publisher, welcomed this project from its first (revived) suggestion and showed the enterprise and determination needed to bring it to print; and her colleagues Louis Mackay and Hugh Brazier have been wholly supportive in their approach to this rather unusual challenge. Mark Myers, marine artist and sailing-ship expert, has been an invaluable source of experience and wisdom, and it is a great pleasure to find a place for his unique paintings to be displayed, over 30 years after they were commissioned, and to acknowledge his extraordinary cooperation over this publication. Dr Keith Carabine, a Conradian scholar and chair of the Joseph Conrad Society of Great Britain, was fascinated to learn of this venture and kind enough to read the manuscript and make a number of most helpful suggestions as to its improvement; he also invited me to address the annual conference of his society. Andrea White of the California State University at Dominguez Hills, current editor of *Conradiana*, immediately supported what she described as this worthy project and was most helpful in enabling me to contact Robert Foulke, a Conradian marine scholar of long standing. Denis Stonham, formerly a senior member of staff of the National Maritime Museum, has been of immense assistance in offering unstinting advice, and I have drawn upon his 'Conrad's command: the barque *Otago*', as published in the *World Ship Review*, no. 42, December 2005. I am also much indebted to Tony Crowley for his expert navigational comments on the same subject.

Mrs Nancie Villiers retains a very clear memory of her late husband's work and intentions, and the completion of this book has been very much a family affair in which my brother Kit and sister Kathie have also participated. Carolyn has shown enormous patience and understanding as I wrestled with the theoretical problems of setting a reefed foresail or finding the location of some of Conrad's more obscure eastern ports, rather than the real and practical demands of building a log-store or painting the house, which a real seaman would have relished, and I am most grateful to her. Finally, Elder Dempster Lines of Liverpool were good enough to give me some experience of life at sea when I was between school and university, a more than usually bewildered young man who needed some time to reflect. My work on the *Freetown* and *Apapa* certainly allowed for this, for the claims of life at sea, as Conrad once said, are still simple and cannot be denied; and I am still reflecting.

Peter Villiers
April 2006

A word about the paintings

The paintings which illustrate this book have emerged, Rip-van-Winkle-like, after a slumber of thirty-one years in a bedroom closet. They were painted in the early months of 1975 at the request of my old captain and mentor Alan Villiers, who talked his publishers into the idea of including in his next book a series of paintings of Joseph Conrad's ships, and helped me throughout with advice on the vessels and events, and with the preliminary drawings. My head was full of Conrad then, so many of the scenes and incidents depicted were simply interpretations on canvas of images that the great Polish writer had brought to life so powerfully in his prose.

Rip van Winkle came to mind when the call came this year to take the paintings out of the closet and see if they would still do for the book. As you know, old Rip was mocked for his antiquated ideas when he awoke after his long sleep, and I was afraid that the paintings – the work of a young artist struggling with his materials and technique – might bring a wry smile to the lips of those who know more recent work of mine. In fact, I was pleasantly surprised to find the pictures, although full of faults in many ways as I'd feared, were also vivid and fresh and told their stories better than I had remembered.

Alan Villiers' writing was an inspiration to me as a schoolboy. By great good fortune he later became a friend and mentor when I was a young man determined to get experience under sail in square-rigged ships. He helped enormously when I began my career as an artist, commissioning paintings now and then and putting my work before his considerable public in the form of illustrations and book jackets, and so I feel a deep and lasting gratitude to the Captain and his family for many kindnesses over many years. This gratefulness continues with thanks to Peter Villiers for taking his father's *Captain Korzeniowski* manuscript in hand and remembering about the paintings. Thanks also to Patricia Eve and Louis Mackay at Seafarer Books, who have taken pains to see them beautifully reproduced, at last, within the covers of this book.

Mark Myers
April 2006

Mont Blanc

I n the late autumn of 1874 a young Pole arrived in the French port of Marseille after a lengthy and tortuous railway journey from Krakow, in what was then Austrian Poland. As a subject of the Russian empire, he travelled on a Russian passport. In Marseille, he was to make contact with a wealthy and influential business family of the town, the Delestangs, whom he hoped would be able to help him in his main ambition: to follow the sea as a career. The young Pole was sixteen years old. He was an orphan. His mother, Evelina Korzeniowska, née Bobrowska, had died in exile in 1865, at the age of 31, when he was a boy of seven. His father, a Polish land-owner, intellectual and patriot called Apollo Korzeniowski, who had played a part in the preparations for the Polish rising against Russia of 1863 and had been exiled thereby, followed her in 1869, when his son was still only eleven. Their only child had been christened Jozef Teodor Konrad Nalecz Korzeniowski; a name he was eventually to change to Joseph Conrad.

Joseph Conrad was born on 3 December 1857 at Berdichev in Podolia, one of the Ukrainian provinces of Poland long under Russian Tsarist rule. Poland had been dismembered by its larger neighbours, Russia, Prussia and Austria, during three consecutive partitions in 1772, 1793 and 1795 – so that by the time Conrad was born it had long officially ceased to exist. However, to remove the name of a nation from the official map does not mean that it will cease to exist in the hearts and minds of its people; and the Poles have always shown a remarkable tenacity in retaining their national identity. Despite the demise of their national independence, Polish history, language and culture remained, and the Poles retained that fierce patriotism by which they are still distinguished. Throughout the nineteenth century, they did not cease to hope for an independent Poland. (This was to come with the collapse of the Tsarist, Austro-Hungarian and Prussian empires at the end of the First World War: in Conrad's lifetime, in fact, and the occasion for his only adult visit to his ancestral home. But we are running ahead of ourselves, and shall return to Conrad's Polish roots later, when he does. For the moment, we are setting the scene.)

Nineteenth-century Poles lived, worked and dreamed of national independence under one of three masters: the Prussians, the Russians, or the Austrians. Which was the best of the three to be ruled by? More appropriate to ask, which was the least unendurable: and the answer to that must be the Austrians, who were the least oppressive, if no less autocratic in intention than their fellow emperors. The Austrian empire (after the *Ausgleich* of 1867, the Austro-Hungarian empire), was a huge and somewhat ramshackle affair, and both multi-racial and multi-cultural by force of circumstance – to say nothing of being multi-religious. Famously, there were both Jewish and Muslim generals in the Austro-Hungarian army, if perhaps not very many, and although Austrian Roman Catholics were top dogs in the empire, members of other faiths, races and ethnic backgrounds *could* make progress – provided that their loyalty was without question.

Such treatment did not apply under Russian rule, where the intention, especially after the rebellion of 1863, was to suppress Polishness altogether. An old Russian proverb says that the only safe frontier is one with Russia on both sides, and the logic of this sentiment was certainly applied in divided Poland.

In practical terms, and whoever their master, Poles faced two options: they could accept the status quo, whilst still hoping to achieve or re-achieve national independence by peaceful means; or they could rebel. Conrad's father, Apollo Korzeniowski, a member of the traditional Polish aristocracy whose family estates had been confiscated, chose the path of rebellion. Apollo scraped a living as a poet, translator and man of letters, but his real interest was in the overthrow of the hated Tsarists. He had married into the Bobrowski family. His wife's brother, Tadeusz Bobrowski – a more influential figure in Conrad's life than his father, perhaps, for Tadeusz was to take on the guardianship of his orphaned nephew when Apollo died – had chosen the more cautious option, and believed in accommodation with the authorities in the hope of long-term change. Consequently, Tadeusz Bobrowski was left alone to retain and manage his estates by the authorities – and to provide the element of security, both financial and otherwise, of which the young Conrad was so much in need.

This difference between father and uncle reflected not only their political views but their general temperaments, as Conrad's uncle was not slow to point out. In Bobrowski's view, the Korzeniowskis, the family into which his sister Eva had married, were distinguished by a sort of reckless impetuosity which often resulted in disaster. The Bobrowskis, on the other hand, were more cautious, more politically skilled, and more adept, reflecting their more phlegmatic approach to life. It is clear, as his uncle not infrequently pointed out to him, that Conrad inherited many of the characteristics of his father, and of the Korzeniowski side of the family. What became apparent, however, is that whatever the defects he may have inherited from a father who had failed in almost every venture that he touched, Joseph Conrad himself was to display a remarkable determination to overcome the obstacles that faced him, first as a sailor and then as an author; and no-one was to be more pleased with his success than his uncle.

In 1861, when Conrad was only three, his parents were arrested by the authorities for revolutionary conspiracy and then banished into exile in northern Russia – their young son to accompany them. (The insurrection that followed the original conspiracy, in Poland in 1863, was a ghastly failure, brutally crushed.) Banishment was a dismal experience for all three, and Eva went on to die at 31, her health and happiness shattered under the harsh conditions of exile.

The effect on Apollo was devastating. As Conrad later wrote, in reflecting upon his childhood, his father was:

> A man of great sensibilities; of exalted and dreamy temperament; with a terrible gift of irony and of a gloomy disposition; withal of strong religious feeling degenerating after the loss of his wife into mysticism touched with despair.[1]

Was Apollo Korzeniowski the model for the world-rejecting father of the main character, Heyst, in Conrad's late novel, *Victory*? Did the relationship between father and son in *Victory* resemble the relationship between the young Conrad and his father, after his mother had died and what remained of the family was suffered to trudge back into Austrian Poland from exile, once the authorities had decided that the once revolutionary zealot Apollo Korzeniowski no longer constituted a threat? It is tempting to imagine that the answer to both questions is in the affirmative. Yes, Apollo Korzeniowski may have been the basis for Axel Heyst's father – the solitary philosopher who despised the world and lived self-sufficient and alone. And yes, the depiction of the father–son relationship between the two Heysts may have been influenced by the widowerhood of Apollo Korzeniowski, transmogrified into fiction by his son: but the case cannot be proved.

What is fiction? That whose purpose is to entertain, provoke and inspire, and whose substance is untrue. But if untrue, it is not necessarily imaginary in the full sense of that word: it may have some basis in reality. No man is an island, said John Donne; and no writer can entirely divorce himself from – himself. It is a risky enterprise to attempt to correlate an author's life, experience and opinions with his fictional output, whether by direct analogy, as it were, or the more fanciful method of psychoanalysis; and there have already been more than enough attempts to do so in the case of Joseph Conrad. Indeed, he himself was to complain of the practice. What he wrote, he said in essence, may have been in part the product of his experience, but it was also the product of his imagination. His characters – Lord Jim, Charlie Marlow, Captain Roderick Anthony, Gentleman Brown, Chief Inspector Heat and all the others – might be based in part upon people he had met, read about, or heard discussed, and might indeed contain elements of Conrad himself. But they were *characters*. They were people he had created. They had a separate and fictional life, independent of their origins. And they were not to be simply equated with historical or contemporary figures, in whole or in part, as some sort of spot-the-ball competition in literary detective work.

Having said all of that, it would be a strange book indeed which made no correlation of any kind between Conrad's life and his fiction – and a much duller one. In what follows, connections will be made where they enhance the text, and with due recognition that they are the connections of the biographer, which might not have been admitted by the author himself. What matters is the quality of Conrad's writing. Are his characters believable? Do his plots make sense? Does he have something to say about the human condition?

---

1. Zdzislaw Najder, *Joseph Conrad: a Chronicle*. Cambridge University Press, Cambridge, 1983, page 28.

Do we enjoy reading him? Would we like to know a little more about his background and experiences, on the understanding that although this may enlarge our understanding of the writer and his work, it does not, at least in any facile sense, 'explain' them? The answers must be yes. And so we return to our story.

From 1869, after the death of his father, Conrad was brought up by his maternal uncle, Tadeusz Bobrowski. Unsurprisingly in view of his early childhood, Conrad was a quiet, introverted and sensitive boy, although talented and intelligent. He showed no very strong ambition until he astonished his uncle by expressing a desire to go to sea; an almost unheard-of ambition in rural Poland. Having formed this aim (perhaps founded at least partly by reading tales of adventure and exploration by such authors as James Fenimore Cooper and Captain Marryat), Conrad kept on pressing his uncle until Bobrowski (an extremely kind, considerate and generous man who continued to help and correspond with Conrad until his death) decided that the best way to accommodate and perhaps hopefully to deflate his nephew's strange whim was actually to give way to it. The question arose, how?

Bobrowski's thoughts turned almost automatically to France. During the whole of the nineteenth century, there was a strong connection between Poland and France. Many Polish exiles had made France their home. The young Conrad had been taught French, was well versed in French literature, and spoke the language, if not like a native, than at least with a certain dash and flair. (Did he know any English, at this stage? The evidence is uncertain. He had heard English spoken, and he had read English texts. But that was supposed to have been in translation. At this stage, there is no evidence that either Conrad or his uncle saw France as a stepping-stone to England. France was a goal in itself.)

France had a strong and independent merchant navy, and an extremely well-organised one. Moreover, Bobrowski knew a particular family in Marseille, the Delestangs, who owned ships, and would be able to allow Conrad to serve on one of them in some sort of supernumerary capacity, and to gain some practical experience of the sea without committing himself too deeply, or for too long. To Marseille he should go. After a year or two at sea, or sowing his wild oats, he might be ready to return to Poland; or, better still, to follow a sensible career in some liberal and enlightened foreign country, not subject to the despotic power of Imperial Russia. Affectionately and regretfully, Bobrowski parted with his young nephew at Krakow railway station.

Not having the power to see into the future, he could have no idea that the nephew of his favourite sister (who had married the dreamy, impractical and romantic Apollo Korzeniowski) would, after an indifferent start, settle down, get into his stride, and go on and become a master mariner in the premier merchant service in the world, the British; nor that this same nephew would go on to become an accomplished and acclaimed writer, and eventually a famous one. Had he been aware that both achievements were in store, he might have been more surprised by the former, for his nephew came of writing and not of sailing stock. However, in 1874 all this was very much in the future.

Mont Blanc in the West Indies

Skimmer of the Sea, coal-laden, in the North Sea

Duke of Sutherland at Circular Quay, Sydney

Loch Etive in fresh weather

Conrad took to Marseille, and the Mediterranean, from the start. It was the first real experience of freedom he had had, in life; and in a glorious and friendly setting.

> The very first whole day I ever spent on salt water was by invitation, in a big half-decked pilot-boat, cruising under close reefs on the look-out, in misty, blowing weather, for the sails of ships and the smoke of steamers ... And many a day and night too did I spend cruising with these rough, kindly men ... Their sea-tanned faces, whiskered or shaved, lean or full, with the intent wrinkled sea-eyes of the pilot-breed, and here and there a thin gold loop at the lobe of a hairy ear, bent over my sea-infancy. (*A Personal Record*, page 123)

Conrad made the acquaintance of the Marseille pilots through a young Frenchman named Baptistin Solang, a friend of the Delestangs charged to look after the even younger Conrad. He was most fortunate to begin his seafaring with such good friends, for beginnings could otherwise be rough. The cruising pilots provided him with a pleasant and interesting introduction to the sea. They were good seamen in their own cruising cutters and small schooners. Their livings depended on reaching a sufficient number of inbound ships before anyone else, and so getting the piloting job inwards, and (they hoped) outwards too. So they cruised far offshore night and day, racing for the distant smoke-smudge or the horizon-breaking pyramid of sail indicating the homeward-bounder: or by night the flare or light showing the same.

After two months in Marseille, and his introduction to the life of the sea through the pilots' cutters, Conrad made his first voyage in a Delestang-owned ship; his first ocean-passage, and the real beginning of his sea-apprenticeship. He signed on the articles of the Delestang 400-ton barque *Mont Blanc*. She was also called a barquentine and schooner at various times, so what her real rig was appears unclear. However, when Conrad signed on she was registered as a barque. A barque or bark is a three-masted sailing ship, square-rigged on her foremast and mainmast and fore-and-aft rigged on her mizzen mast, to make her more manoeuvrable. It is also possible to have a four-masted or even a five-masted barque, such as the twentieth-century German ship *Potosi*, one of the greatest sailing ships ever built. Whether the barque has three, four or five masts, it is only the aftermost mast that is rigged fore-and-aft. A barquentine and brigantine, by contrast, are square-rigged only on the foremast, the most forward mast, and may be fore-and-aft-rigged on one or more following masts. A schooner is not square-rigged at all, but is rigged wholly fore-and-aft, like a modern yacht (unless she be a tops'l schooner – see the glossary at the end of this book for further terms and information).

A word about signing on. The *Mont Blanc* was a registered cargo-carrying vessel, and by law all persons carried aboard such a ship in whatever capacity were required to sign the ship's articles of agreement. These accounted for their presence on board, gave a proper contractual status to those who were crew, and prevented (in theory, at least) masters from assisting wanted criminals or other escapers from leaving Marseille or any other port by sea.

Conrad, who had no maritime experience and who was very far from the average merchant naval recruit, was signed on the articles of the *Mont Blanc* as a passenger. Thus any time he spent on this ship would be of no value to him as a professional seaman, since it could not be used to count towards sea-time. Sea-time was time spent at sea (or even in port) on the articles of a ship in a recognised capacity as apprentice, ordinary seaman or able-bodied seaman. The British merchant service required four years' sea-time to be achieved before one could sit for the second mate's ticket, and the French had a similar system. There was no requirement for the aspiring ship's officer to serve an apprenticeship, and many successful candidates did not do so. What was essential was practical experience in working a ship. Formal study, or rather cramming, came later.

Conrad at this stage may simply have been experimenting with the sea, or unaware of the requirements of sea-time: whichever the case, his status on the *Mont Blanc* was in fact to cause him difficulties when he did sit for his second mate's ticket. But that was very much in the future.

The *Mont Blanc* sailed from Marseille for Martinique on 11 December 1874 with Conrad aboard as passenger, and her arrival there is recorded on 26 February of the following year, 1875. This is an ocean passage of 67 days: she was 21 years old and in no hurry. Once clear of the Mediterranean and the Straits of Gibraltar, this was almost an ideal trade-winds run for the first voyager, for northerly winds could be relied on to blow the little barque to the zone of the northeast trades in the tropics which, with any luck, took her right to the West Indies in that most pleasant of all sailing – the trade winds. Day after day the silent, shapely vessel skimmed along with the warm wind filling all her sails and the whisper of the roll-over sea at her cutwater rising to song as the sun climbed slowly and the wind strengthened, her speed picked up and her wake increased, and the great seabirds soared on the up-draughts from her sails. This was exhilarating and extremely pleasant, the ideal introduction to the seafaring life – perhaps misleading too, for ships do not stay in trade winds.

The very effectiveness of the northeast trade in sending the little ship hurrying to the westwards was equally effective in preventing her return that way to Europe: for this, she had to go by another, much harder way. She had to get to the north beyond the trade-wind belt to pick up westerlies – working across the baffling zones of variables in the process and often finding the westerlies most uncertain, for the circulatory movement of the equatorial air which gave such a measure of constancy in the trades did not apply further north. No matter: there was the Gulf Stream to help shove ships from the Caribbean towards the north, and a useful drift of the same warm water eastwards towards Europe. The Atlantic's westerlies could be (and often were) very strong when they blew: the six-knot grace of the trades became a headlong, ten-knot rush, the barque wet, pitching, rolling, and hard to hold. Usually she had a heavy cargo of West Indies logs, which filled much of the hold and main deck alike, heavily chained down but making the gear more difficult to work and the decks hard to get round.

The *Mont Blanc* was 55 days sailing back to Marseille, where she arrived on 23 May 1875. This compared with 67 days outwards in the quieter trade winds. The whole voyage, to the West Indies and back, must have been a near-perfect introduction for Conrad to the deep-sea sailing-ship sea life, and the six weeks at Martinique were pleasant too.

After a month or so in Marseille, Conrad signed on the *Mont Blanc* again for another West Indies voyage, this time as an apprentice – *pilotin*, as the French had it. Any apprentice lived aft, acted as a junior member of the afterguard, had clearly defined duties including the care of food and wines (*real* care of these things, not perfunctory supervision of the allocation of pound and pint of trash and the limejuice issue), made his own contribution to the crew's welfare and had a good opportunity to learn, too. For he observed the ship from aft, the place of command; he mixed with and was accepted by the officers as one of them, at least in aspiration. Such young officer-aspirants were called *pilotins*, and were not normally greatly respected by the tough mariners for'ard, reared to the sea. These often called them *fils-de-Papa* – sons of a Somebody (privileged young gentlemen) – or, more familiarly, 'captains of the fowl house'. The afterguard of French sailing ships took their food seriously, like sensible men, and a good ship's fare at sea included chicken for the midday meal aft on Thursdays and Sundays (and reasonable food properly prepared on other days, too). It took a good chicken ranch to keep the standard going, and a reliable man (or boy) to look after so important a matter.

Conrad's second voyage, which was to Martinique again, and Haiti, took six months – much the same pleasant westward trade-wind romp as on the first voyage. But homewards was a very different matter. The ship was deeply laden with a logwood cargo (dye-woods, probably) bound for Le Havre, and it was winter. She did not sail from Cap Haitian until 1 November and reached Le Havre two days before Christmas. November and December are rough months in the North Atlantic and the 23-year-old wooden barque leaked – 'fully, generously, over-flowingly, like a basket,' wrote Conrad – and the heavy logs were a straining cargo. Having to sail to the English Channel instead of the Straits of Gibraltar made a big difference too, for obviously the ship had to sail much further to the north, make a difficult landfall and sail up-channel in poor visibility with hell's own wind behind her. When she reached Le Havre (for she was a strong old barque and could scarcely have leaked quite as much as Conrad said or she would have been fitted with a windmill pump) he was in such a hurry to leave that he left his trunk at Le Havre station – not the first *pilotin* to do that!

Conrad stayed ashore six months before shipping out again. During this period he managed to spend a lot of money (thereby upsetting his uncle) and no doubt greatly enjoyed the delights that Marseille had to offer. When he chose to sign on again, Conrad had one year of foreign-going sea service behind him (disregarding his time as a 'passenger'), and was thereby entitled to sign on as an ordinary seaman. But, in July 1876, he signed on the articles of the 430-ton Delestang barque *Saint Antoine* as steward. This was professional nonsense, and appears so bizarre that it may have been done simply so that authority would be less likely to ask any awkward questions about Conrad's presence on the ship, and his nationality.

Conrad was now nearly nineteen, and his life was just approaching a potential crisis (at this stage perhaps more apparent to the far-sighted and practical Tadeusz Bobrowski in Poland than to the young adventurer in France). The problem was one of nationality. Conrad could not continue to serve in the French merchant navy without becoming a French citizen. The French merchant service was a well-recognised national asset. On reaching the age of twenty, a seaman in it received his first training as a naval reservist. For this he had to be legally and incontestably French. Thereafter, he was documented and registered, a trained naval reservist as well as a merchant seaman. (For his liability to national naval service, and as some recompense for the time spent preparing for it, the French seaman enjoyed the privilege of a pension at the age of fifty, which put him in a different class to most other merchant seamen, and especially the British.)

What was to prevent the obvious solution – Conrad becoming French? Just one simple fact: the Russian nationality with which he had been officially saddled at birth. Poland had ceased to exist as an independent country in 1795, and Conrad was subject to Russian laws. He had sailed in French ships without the permission of the Russian consul. All sorts of problems might have been raised by his applying to the Russian government for permission to serve in the French merchant navy: Conrad had avoided them by not applying for permission. If he now applied to the Russians to become a Frenchman, he faced the prospect of being conscripted into the Russian army to do his military service instead; and, as the son of a political convict, he could serve twenty-five years in the ranks. Therefore, to attempt to obtain French nationality was much too risky; he would have to leave the French merchant service before long.

The *Saint Antoine* sailed from Marseille with Conrad aboard – the crew list exists – on 3 July 1876; was at St Pierre six weeks later (another fine trade-winds passage), and wandered round the Caribbean and the old Spanish Main – calling at Colon, Cartagena, Puerto Cabello, La Guaira, St Thomas in the Danish West Indies, Port-au-Prince in Haiti, before sailing for Marseille just after the autumnal equinox – a rough season in those parts. Her homewards cargo was logwood and sugar – another heavy gut-full – and she was over 80 days making the passage east, though she had been careened and the bottom cleaned in Haiti. She arrived back in Marseille on 15 February 1877 and Conrad was paid off.

It is impossible to know for certain exactly what the *Saint Antoine* carried in addition to her legitimate cargo, but there is a strong suspicion that she was involved in gun-running. These were years of grave unrest in some Central American republics, and the dominions of Spain. Gun-running was a serious but often profitable business, and there was at least one expert at it in the *Saint Antoine*; the mate, the Corsican Dominic Cervoni. Conrad appears to have admired him and learned a good deal from him, and not just about gun-running. Cervoni was to be the model for *Nostromo*, the resolute and capable 'capataz de cargadores', or chief of stevedores, in Conrad's novel of the same name. The novel is set in a mythical South American republic; Conrad's experiences gained in the *Saint Antoine*, short in time as they were, would have helped to give him the background for his literary creation, which he wrote two decades later.

In his reminiscences, Conrad hints at having been involved in illegal activities on the *Saint Antoine*, but, naturally enough, does not state exactly what he did. In any case, it is safe to conclude that however much his service as 'steward' on the *Saint Antoine* may have helped his subsequent literary career, it was of very little value to him in his career in the merchant navy.

The time had come for him to change to the British merchant service if he were seriously to make a career at sea. The British merchant flag had considerable advantages for Conrad, of which the chief was that British merchant seamen, unlike adult French, were neither then (nor for many years afterward) properly documented: indeed, it could be argued that they were not really documented at all, for their only written record of a life at sea might be a handful of more or less legible discharge certificates, giving the barest official account of their time afloat. The British merchant service, with the success of steam (very largely developed in the United Kingdom) needed seamen in large and growing numbers. So long as these could be found conscious and preferably sober, nobody cared where they came from; and whilst a minimal record was kept of their service at sea, in other ways they were entirely free: free to starve, drown or prosper under the Red Ensign, as character and circumstances allowed.

Drown at sea, many of them unfortunately did; and the record of their deaths, and the miserably few possessions they may have left behind to be auctioned for the benefit of any next of kin, can make equally miserable reading. Alan Villiers made a painstaking study of the sailing-ship logs from the last days of sail, and records the vicissitudes of life and death at sea in the words of the official chroniclers of the day: the ships' masters who were responsible for maintaining the ships' logs.[2] He discusses the general conditions of life at sea in the merchant navy of Conrad's day in the appendix at the end of this book.

Before Conrad left France, however, there is a period to be accounted for. The time between Conrad's ceasing to serve on the *Saint Antoine* and his leaving France is the most mysterious period of his life. He wrote about it in some detail in his reminiscences. His experiences then appear to have formed the basis for one of his last novels, *The Arrow of*

---

2. Alan Villiers, *The War with Cape Horn*. Hodder and Stoughton, London, 1971.

Gold – which he claimed to be based on truth, although many of his biographers have disputed this. Finally, his uncle's letters relating to Conrad's activities during this period still exist, and can be analysed. Despite all this, it is not at all clear what really happened.

If we accept Conrad's account in *The Mirror of the Sea* as being at least partly true, during this period Conrad formed a syndicate with three other young men, an American, an Englishman and a Frenchman, and ran guns to the Carlist faction in Spain. To make the story even better, we learn that there was a lady involved – the mysterious Dona Rita, who

> was perpetually rushing off to Paris to interview in the interests of the cause – Por el Rey! For she was a Carlist, and of Basque blood at that, and with something of the lioness in the expression of her courageous face (especially when she let her hair down), and with the volatile little soul of a sparrow dressed in fine Parisian feathers, which had the trick of coming off disconcertingly at unexpected moments. (*Mirror of the Sea*, page 160)

The syndicate purchased a small craft named the *Tremolino* (whose rig was variously described). She was clearly an extremely fast vessel, and made a great impression on the young Conrad. This is now he describes her:

> She who was my cradle in those years had been built on the River of Savona by a famous builder of boats, was rigged in Corsica by another good man, and was described on her papers as a 'tartane' of 60 tons. In reality, she was a true balancelle, with two short masts raking forward and two curved yards, each as long as her hull; a true child of the Latin Lake, with a spread of two enormous sails resembling the pointed wings on a sea-bird's tender body, and herself, like a bird indeed, skimming rather than sailing the seas. (*Mirror of the Sea*, page 156)

She was commanded by the ruthless, sardonic and equally impressive Dominic Cervoni, with Conrad acting as a kind of marine overseer and organiser: the sea-going member of the syndicate, as he called himself. Things went well for a while, until eventually disaster struck: Cervoni had to ram the *Tremolino* onto rocks and sink her to prevent her being seized by the Spanish coastguard, apparently because Cervoni's nephew Cesar had betrayed them to the authorities. Conrad's account of the whole affair is given in *The Mirror of the Sea*, pages 157 to 183, his style a mixture of the romantic and the ironic, for this is an older man reflecting back upon the excitements and transgressions of his youth; and like his father, Conrad had a 'terrible gift of irony'. He tells us not only that Dominic Cervoni murdered his nephew for betraying the cause, but also that ten thousand francs in gold – gold for which Conrad was accountable, and which was intended to finance the Royalist cause – was lost as Cesar sank and drowned with the stolen coins in a belt around his waist.

Well! What a story! Youth, adventure, seduction and betrayal: a heady brew. How much of it was true? We do not know; but we may infer that the *Tremolino* and all her adventures were grist to the mill of the nascent writer, Joseph Conrad.

In the meantime, the kindly and accommodating landowner Tadeusz Bobrowski had learned nothing of his wayward nephew's involvement in the Carlist cause, but was alarmed to discover that the young Joseph had plunged heavily into debt; that he was unable to return to sea in a French vessel, as French regulations had caught up with him; that in any case he had quarrelled with the Delestangs; and, most alarming and worrying of all, Bobrowski was informed by telegram that Conrad had been wounded. He went to Marseille to see what had happened and found Conrad still alive and recovering from a bullet-wound in the chest. He later wrote to a friend that Conrad had tried to shoot himself, largely because he had made an utter mess of his financial affairs and was in debt to the tune of 6,000 francs, this after he had already overspent his allowance before and had been seriously admonished by his uncle. Bobrowski redeemed his nephew's debts again.

Conrad makes no mention of having attempted to shoot himself, and the possibility arises that he was wounded in a duel. In any case, he had been sowing his wild oats with a vengeance. Whatever the truth of the business of the *Tremolino*, she was now gone; the Carlists had lost in Spain; Conrad had no future in the French merchant navy; and it was time for him to try another country's service.

On 24 April 1878 he signed on the *Mavis*, a freighter of 760 tons, of London (Captain Munnings). He was noted in the articles as an ordinary seaman, without pay. This was clearly a special arrangement made with the aim of conveying Conrad to England. Indeed, it transpired that Conrad had had to pay the captain 400 francs in cash (provided by Bobrowski) to obtain this passage.

The *Mavis* wandered to England from Marseille by way of Constantinople and the Sea of Azov with her cargo of coal; a small and undistinguished steamer, and a small and undistinguished beginning of Conrad's career in the British merchant service.

When the *Mavis* eventually reached Lowestoft Conrad left, rushed down to London, and wrote to his uncle asking for a further 500 francs. For once, his long-suffering and faithful uncle was really annoyed. Originally Conrad had given him to understand that he 'fancied' the English steamer, and had intended to stay at least some time in her; now he had wasted the good of giving 400 francs, a considerable sum, to her master, thereby displaying what his uncle considered the usual Nalecz Korzeniowski characteristics of recklessness and extravagance, as if he had learned nothing in France at all. 'I did not send you where you are now,' he wrote to Conrad in London. 'I agreed to your sailing in an English vessel but not to your staying in England, travelling to London and wasting money there! I can give you only one piece of advice. Arrange your budget within the allowance I now give you for I will give no more. Don't pretend to be a rich young gentleman and wait for someone else to pull your chestnuts from the fire ... DO something: earn something!'

Poor Conrad. But it was excellent advice, and necessary. So Conrad did something. He signed in the *Skimmer of the Sea* for the derisory 'wage' of one shilling a month.

Skimmer of the Sea

Aknowledgeable seaman might well ask why, with surely a wide selection of sailing merchantmen to serve in, Conrad should have chosen the *Skimmer of the Sea*. She was a humble, unpretentious and hard-working little North Sea barquentine of 320 tons, employed in carrying coal from Newcastle to Lowestoft. She carried a very small crew, all of whom would be expected to help in loading and unloading that coal – dirty, hard, repetitive labour (for each trip down the North Sea only lasted a few days on average, and there was much shovelling to be done at both ends of it). This was altogether a very different sort of sea life to the one Conrad had first known in France, in his cruising off Marseille in pilot-cutters, voyaging to the West Indies in the trade winds, and gun-running to Spain under the romantic and authoritative guidance of Dominic Cervoni.

And yet the *Skimmer of the Sea* was a good choice for Conrad. Her rig was of the same family as the two small French square-riggers in which he had already sailed. He knew the ropes and the sequence of orders aboard that type of vessel. The run of the rigging and the hanging of it were all standard. So was the manner in which sail was set, reefed and taken in. Conrad would know what to do and when, aboard the *Skimmer*, and would be an immediately useful member of the crew, even if he did not understand every order that was shouted. All this would make it that much simpler for him to make the big changeover from French to English sailing-ship language. Apart from that, the *Skimmer of the Sea* had carried a few passengers in her time, so Conrad would have had a small cabin of his own – a considerable advantage in those days, when a ship's forecastle was usually crowded, international and rough, though not actually squalid; the senior AB's would see that decent standards of cleanliness were kept. Conrad as 'passenger', *pilotin* and 'steward' in the French ships *Mont Blanc* and *Saint Antoine* would not have lived in the forecastles, but in his own cabin; he was able to continue this custom in the *Skimmer*. Conrad had a contact in Lowestoft, a Mr Karch, known to his uncle; it was probably he who arranged for the young Pole to ship in the *Skimmer* after Conrad had indicated what sort of ship he was seeking.

Finally, his choice may have been influenced, whether consciously or sub-consciously, by an association of names. James Fenimore Cooper, the American writer of adventure stories, had written a novel called *The Skimmer of the Sea*s, or *The Water Witch*. Conrad may have read it as a boy, for he was a great reader of adventure stories. Here was an actual ship named the *Skimmer of the Sea*. Coincidence? Presumably – and certainly not enough to influence the ordinary merchant sailor in his choice of ship. But Joseph Conrad, from the beginning to the end of his merchant service career, was no ordinary merchant sailor.

Any seaman of those days would have known at a glance that the *Skimmer* had begun her sea life not as a rigged-down barquentine, but as a barque (see glossary). The ship had been defrauded of half her effective square-sail area: all the square sails formerly on the main, i.e. the main course itself, one (maybe two) tops'ls above it, a topgallant-sail, and a royal above that. Compared with this sort of nobly traditional spread, the gaff-and-boom main and triangular rag of a gaff tops'l above it could be somewhat inadequate substitutes. Nevertheless the *Skimmer of the Sea* had the look of a deepwater wandering barque about her, and Conrad would have been susceptible to this. Throughout his maritime career he was to show a talent for choosing ships of character: the odd, the interesting, the unusual. He saw poetry and beauty in the classic lines of vessels, where the less discerning saw only poverty and rust.

For the *Skimmer of the Sea* deserved her name. She had begun her sea life over twenty years before Conrad saw her, as a deepwater barque; and she had ranged the world as cargoes offered, to Chile, the Pacific coast of Mexico, Brazil, Australia, with her full share of excitement, romance and suffering.

Her maiden voyage in 1855 had taken her out of Liverpool with an all-British crew of twelve under her master Robert Hogg, aged 36, bound for Valparaiso around the Horn. The official log and – most unusually – the deck log of this voyage still exist, because Captain Hogg added his deck log to the documents he was required to return and sent them both bound in the one large blue book. (They are in the keeping of the National Maritime Museum in Greenwich.) This makes the *Skimmer* very well documented, at least on that voyage. The deck log is exceptionally well kept, obviously from the watch-keepers' slates, as was the custom then. It shows that the little barque took the round voyage in her stride, a 20,000-mile stride at least, for it was from Liverpool direct to Valparaiso, then to Guayamas and Mazatlan, and back to Liverpool with two roundings of the Horn. The crew were all British, which was unusual in a deepwater British vessel in those days; the forecastle usually contained a thoroughly international community. The *Skimmer of the Sea* was a Great Yarmouth ship and there was local pride in her. For so long a voyage, crew turnover is slight – a sign of the well-run ship. There are only two changes recorded.

If it seems incredible that a minute barque of some 350 tons register could take on so considerable a commercial voyage or pay a dividend when she did, it must be remembered that a well-built small wooden ship rode more safely and could be far less hazardous in great seas than the 2,000- or 3,000-ton steel monsters which succeeded her, for the big fellows smashed into the sea, their main-deck awash, and the sea smashed over them. The little wooden barque rode buoyant and yielding, slipping along when the storms were not looking, working through the doldrums on the flap of her sails while the big metal wagon might sit there sweating in her own reflection. As for the economics, nobody then (except Brunel) thought in terms of freights and goods moving about the earth in terms of tens of thousands of tons, or even just thousands – even one thousand was a lot. It was not that kind of world, and few imagined then that such a world was likely ever to be needed, or developed.

The *Skimmer* could pay quite well on her small freights. Her capital costs were extremely low – a very few thousand pounds of initial investment for ship, sails, rigging, boats and all. Her own people loaded her efficiently and worked her cargoes out at the voyage-end as crew, and their pay covered this. The whole payroll on that first voyage was less than £40 a month, and the simple feeding cost little. Port dues were slight or non-existent, for she went to anchorages, not expensive built berths. She hired no tugs even when they were available: she could sail, kedge or warp herself along in and out of most ports, or be towed out with her own boat if she could not slip in and out under easy sail. As a small barque, she was a very handy vessel: the two masts of square sails were most effective stopping, swinging and manoeuvring agents as well as her means of forward way. Their handling was in the sight of all her crew, under control of the master, who could swing her like a top, back her or fill her, do anything but push her sideways, with no stress at all.

It was a matter of simple arithmetic to work out her voyage economics, barring accidents; and once she was at sea, money meant nothing. She advanced under sail and was operated by her crew with no outgoings. The food was simple – salted meat in barrels, stockfish, hard biscuits, hard peas for pea soup, strong tea and weak coffee, and limejuice to keep the scurvy away. The ports she sailed to then were small, too, without facilities either for handling large quantities of anything or for the fast turn-round of impatient steamships. No wonder, then, that such small ships remained at sea into Conrad's day and beyond, even if some were to suffer the indignity of being reduced to colliers.

Conrad signed the articles of the *Skimmer of the Sea* on 11 July 1878, more than three years after he had first gone to sea in the *Mont Blanc* from Marseille in December 1874. But he was still officially an 'ordinary seaman'. A serious professional merchant seaman should have become an able seaman in that time, but Conrad had been described as a 'passenger' and 'steward' in the French barques, which would not have allowed him to qualify.

He stayed in the *Skimmer* for two and a half months, signing off again at the home port of Lowestoft on 23 September the same year. During those ten and a half weeks the barquentine made six round voyages to Newcastle, hauling back at least 2,400 tons of coal. This was good going. She must have been a reasonably good sailor, and William Cook, her uncertificated master, handled her well.

But it was a workhorse's life, perhaps particularly rough on that unpaid and unskilled travelling coal-heaver who signed on the articles as Konrad Korzeniowski (it might be de Korzeniowski) aged 20, of Poland. The derisory shilling-a-month 'wage' he signed for was usually not even offered at the pay-off table. It just about bought the seaman's matches which he was expected to supply for relighting side-lights, stern-light if any, and binnacles when these blew out. The ship's articles show a full crew of eight only, including Captain William Cook (his pay is listed as £6 a month), and his mate, Arthur Chandler, who signed for £5 and ten shillings monthly, a mere ten shillings more than the two able seamen received. These would be good and faithful able seamen, one in each of the two watches, crammed with local knowledge even to the ability to identify the village church bells they could hear from seawards, and the ways of the coastwise sailing-ship sea and some at least of the herds of cows on prominent sea-cliff fields, for all local knowledge could help in fog. The four others aboard were under 21, Conrad at 20 the oldest. He was the only foreigner. This would have been unique in the *Skimmer*'s deep-sea days: but coasting ships attracted a different type of man – the home-born local, not the international outcast of the deep-sea forecastles. How Conrad understood their broad Norfolk speech, only the Lord knows. At least the fact that he had little spoken English at the time – and that little bookish and largely academic – would have made no difference.

He seems to have brought luck to the *Skimmer*. Six passages made in the ten and a half weeks while he was aboard and signed on her articles was very good; in the next 14 weeks she made only eight more passages. She wasted no time in port. Her work was to keep the coal stocks of owner Joseph Saul at maximum, especially during the summer when there was a build-up for winter. During at least the two worst winter months she did not operate. Each voyage – 'trip', rather, for Lowestoft to Newcastle and back was hardly a voyage – she hurried up the North Sea as fast as wind and weather allowed, by as direct and safe route as possible, from the harbour mouth of Lowestoft to the Tyne. At least Lowestoft, as the most easterly port in England, gave a ship the chance of keeping a safe offing from the land (so long as the wind was not blowing directly on-shore) as soon as she was past the hump of Norfolk. So she would sail well out to sea from the Wash, away from the busy fishermen of Grimsby and Hull past Spurn Head, clear of Flamborough Head and Whitby – James Cook's home port (Conrad was to pick up his tracks later thousands of miles from there) – past the Hartlepools and Sunderland and into the Tyne.

It was a busy coast, crowded with shipping – far more ships in the 1870s and 1880s than later, because they were all so small then – but a great many were still wind-blown and could keep out of one another's way more readily than the later single-screwed, low-powered vessels. Most had at least some square sail: many were brigs, barquentines, or little barques. Square sails can swing a ship fast or bring her up all-standing very quickly in the hands of any good master. In those waters, bad masters drowned.

So it went, on the shuttle-like progress of the hard-working *Skimmer*. into the Tyne and straight to the familiar coal-berth, tip, or whatever it was, hatches open, everything ready, though a turn to load might have to be waited for. The Tyne was a busy river. As soon as her 400 tons or so of coal was poured, pitched, dropped or flung into her, away again she sped down the busy river for the North Sea, the crew shovelling coal off the decks into the hold where it belonged, trimming it under the ship's beams away from the hatches to make room for the maximum cargo below. Coal at the tips spilled copiously on the *Skimmer*'s decks as she filled: there was plenty to do as she picked her way downriver under easy sail. Once outside, she leapt southwards again (or if the wind were light, dribbled), to make the best run possible.

Of course, it wasn't all hurry – not by any means. Little ships had to wait their turn to load in port and for God's wind at sea, for they must sail as the Lord allowed. If an easterly gale blew home into the Tyne they could wait there for days eager for a slant, just weather-bound. Calm was no use to them either: power among them was unknown, unmissed and unthought of.

Trimming the coal as loaded was rough but at least 'downhill' work: the same small crew worked it out again at Lowestoft, and that meant shovelling the lot into sacks or baskets – uphill work, and plenty of it. For power to lift the baskets to the dockside there was a perambulating cart-horse on the quay, or a hand-operated dolly-winch on deck – roundy-go-roundy, back-breaking stuff, more fit for galley slaves than the scion of the Nalecz Korzeniowskis.

The horse was harnessed to the end of a simple hoisting whip which led through blocks at yardarm and mainstay into the hold. Old Dobbin knew to a nicety the precise number of steps necessary to hoist a basket, and stepped that out and no more. He learned the ship's bells fast, too; at 8 bells noon he quit, on the last double stroke, for he knew that that was feeding time. He knew his work: the tough life of the little *Skimmer* was a fast teacher. Nobody had to drive him.

It is often stated that Conrad knew little if any English when he disembarked from the *Mavis* at Lowestoft, but this can hardly have been so. In the first place, he had grown up in a thoroughly cosmopolitan household. Failure as a manager and rebel as his father Apollo undoubtedly proved to be, no-one questioned his skills as a *litterateur* and translator, who had translated some of the English classics into Polish. The boy Jozef had from a very early age helped and worked with his lonely father, and may have learnt some literary English.

Secondly, Conrad writes with pride of his membership of a Royalist 'syndicate' when a young man in Marseille. The syndicate included an American and an Englishman. Were they so linguistically set that *all* conversation was in French, Catalan or Spanish, when English was the common language of half the group? Or did the young, intelligent and intellectually curious Pole begin to experiment with this new language, as a part of his late adolescence?

Finally, on the long voyage from Marseille to England via Constantinople and Yeusk, it is improbable that he could have communicated much with anyone aboard without learning and using at least some English. Seamen did not need all that much and were not accustomed to a high standard. Apparently Conrad had learnt at least enough English to have a row with Captain Munnings about the 400 franc 'premium' he had had to pay for his passage, when he left.

Whatever English he astonished the mariners of the *Skimmer* with when he first joined – Conrad's spoken English was never perfect in pronunciation, far from it, and when under any stress it could become almost incomprehensible in the early seafaring days – he had a good deal more when he left, particularly in the vital 'lingo' of the sea, a technical language or jargon, in the best sense of that word, which he writes about with both admiration and respect in *The Mirrror of the Sea*. Conrad was the son of a scholar, and appreciated the proper use of language. On a ship, everything has its name, and every order has a clear and unmistakable meaning. It has been said by more than one commentator that the sea provided the young Pole with a sense of purpose, a form of comradeship, and indeed a set of values, which his life as the orphaned son of an exiled Polish revolutionary had previously lacked. Perhaps it did. Conrad was a complex person, and the sea would have fulfilled many purposes in his life.

On 25 September Conrad left by train from Lowestoft for London, by way of Ipswich and Colchester. Within a couple of weeks, he had signed on the articles of another British sailing ship at the same contemptuous 'wage' of one shilling a month. He must have needed money, for the greater part of the year's Bobrowski allowance had gone already on the *Mavis* premium, on life in London for the wasted month between his arrival in Lowestoft and return to join the *Skimmer of the Sea*, in necessary living expenses afterwards, and at least an outfit or two of warm sea clothing.

In later years, as a distinguished (and shore-bound) writer, he was to look back on his service in the *Skimmer* with great affection. Those days, however, were still far ahead for the young Polish seaman, who needed to make his way forward in a foreign merchant service and a foreign land.

Duke of Sutherland

Conrad was now ready to take on a deepwater square-rigger, one of the big ships (1,000 tons or more) in the Australian trade. He now knew the square-rigger's gear and standard orders in seafaring English reasonably well, and the British watch-keeping system and sea-style. He had to learn to convert the elementary knowledge gained in a small barquentine for use in a large full-rigged ship, but this should not take long. One square-rigged mast was very much like another. But how was he to find a suitable ship, and obtain a berth in her?

Obviously the first thing to do was to travel from Lowestoft to London, Britain's major port, and this Conrad did; but it did not solve his problem. It was very difficult, if not impossible, for a seaman to get round to apply for a berth aboard ship himself, in a vast port like London where so many ships were locked away in more or less inaccessible docks, private and guarded, strung out behind miles of tidal riverside all without access by public transport.

The signing-on halls, dignified by the name of Shipping Offices, were the places officially designed as authorised for the engagement of new crews of deepwater ships before a voyage, and for signing off (with their pay, if any) the survivors and others who had joined along the way at the end of the voyage. In the halls alone were ships' crews officially allowed to be engaged – 'signed on' was the expression. It was supposed to be organised and efficient, but to frequent such a place in the vague hope of finding a berth in a ship there and then was a hopeless proceeding, particularly in bad times.

When the shipless sought a berth, it was always 'bad times'. What the seaman really had to do was to know about ships signing on before they did so, and to be there then in good time, with his papers. He knew about ships from other seamen, the talk of the trade. He lived ashore among other seamen, mixed with them, and in fact scarcely knew anyone else, except a few harlots very temporarily.

If he had no home (often the case) he lived in a seaman's establishment among his own kind, almost as much cut off as in a ship at sea. But he did get advance news of jobs in such places (which were often run very well: one speaks from experience), of ships signing on, so that he might make his way aboard beforehand with his discharge book or perhaps just a discharge sheet from the ship he had recently left, and apply to the mate or master. These were glad enough to know of good men, for almost invariably the ship's crew they had arrived with were dispersed with the four winds within a day of paying off. It cost money to keep good men by a ship in port. 'Liners' might do it, tramps not. It was the best sailing ships' trade that the successful steamships took first, the 'line' trades. By 1880 there were not so many sailing-ship lines left under the British flag, for much of their trade had gone to steam.

Conrad's solution to the problem was to use an agent, a go-between, a 'fixer', for he knew no ship's company who had paid off with him (the *Skimmer*'s lads stayed with their ship) and no-one in shipping, or in London at all. And he had never had to pound the waterfront in France. The only sort of agent available to him in London was a man who arranged premium apprenticeships for youths of good family, sons of the manse or of minor civil servants, misfit school-teachers and that sort, who thought they wanted to go to sea as a career but had neither knowledge nor connections to help them in that strangely difficult ambition. Such an agent had placed a small advertisement in a local Suffolk weekly newspaper, and Conrad noted it. So his first quest in London was for this agent's office in Fenchurch Street.

The agent may well have been taken aback by Conrad, for this strange young foreigner would quickly have made it clear that he sought a berth in a big ship's half-deck (the traditional apprentice's quarters) but did not wish to pay a premium for the privilege. In other words, he wished simply to be shipped as an ordinary seaman – but with the advantage of living in the half-deck rather than the crowded, uncomfortable and noisy forecastle, where he would have found it very hard to study for his second mate's ticket.

The disadvantage of the apprentices' half-deck was that it was often in the wettest part of a deep-sea ship; but Conrad would not yet have known this. Had he known, he might have considered using his three years' sea-time and signing on as an AB (able-bodied seaman, one stage up on ordinary seaman), to be paid about three pounds a month – not very much, but an improvement on being an unpaid apprentice. There were aspiring ships' officers in the forecastles of some ships, as in the half-deck. However, the agent would not have been able to obtain an AB's post for Conrad, had he suggested it.

In big sailing-ship ports abroad such as San Francisco, New York, several of the Puget Sound ports, and Sydney and Newcastle, New South Wales, such 'agents' were in operation. Since these men made a living from supplying crews to outward-bound ships, their activities naturally included stealing the crews of inward-bounders to have a commodity to sell. They were helped in this practice by the masters of some British ships, especially if the ships faced a long wait for the next freight. Ship-masters in sail were very poorly paid, and British seamen had no entitlement to any wages at all before their voyage was completed. Therefore, stolen or deserting seamen had to leave their balance of pay on the ship's ledger. The master kept the ledger and the slop-chest too. He made all entries, which did not even have to be counter-signed. Other abuses were also possible.

The agent approached by Conrad – probably some general and perfectly law-abiding small-scale broker – explained to Conrad that if he wanted to go to sea as a passenger or indentured apprentice, then it would be proper for an agent to make introductions in the usual manner. But for him to even appear to supply a working seaman was impossible. That was known as 'crimping', and there were laws against it – presumably intended to prevent men who did *not* wish to go to sea from being 'Shanghaied', or losing part or all of their signing-on money to the agent. Like many such laws, they did not necessarily achieve the effect they intended and, in seeking to remedy one abuse, created another.

However, there was a solution to the problem. Daniel Louttit, owner of the *Duke of Sutherland*, was one of the few ship-owners opposed to the premium apprenticeship system. His ship had a half-deck for apprentices where he placed lads of better family and education than the ordinary foc's'l hands. These young men signed on articles as indentured apprentices in the normal way, but without paying premiums. In fact, Louttit's generosity may have been more sensible than philanthropic. The *Duke of Sutherland* proclaimed herself to be a wool-clipper, but she was getting old, and was finding it more difficult to make fast passages. Steamers were cutting in seriously on the wool-carrying trade from Australia to England. The *Duke of Sutherland* might soon be forced out of commission; when that happened, Louttit had no other ships to which he could transfer his indentured apprentices, and so he would be obliged to pay back any premiums he might have obtained. So he did not charge premiums, and contented himself with free labour from his apprentices.

As the *Duke of Sutherland* would be about a year on her voyage, Conrad should have a year's Bobrowski allowance to collect at the end of it – 2,000 francs. Conrad (still as Korzeniowski, as he was to remain throughout his merchant service) signed the *Sutherland*'s articles on 12 October 1878, the twenty-sixth crew member (a good crew for a thousand-tonner) at his nominal wage of one shilling a month, for the coming voyage London to Sydney and thence the usual sailing-ship options – which meant to anywhere on earth accessible by sea between latitude 75 degrees north and 60 degrees south for a period not to exceed three years. This was to allow the ship to go on to China for tea (if a charter offered, which was extremely improbable, for Suez had been open then for nearly ten years) or California or India or Java or Chile or anywhere else where useful cargo might be found, if there were not enough wool and general in Sydney or Melbourne.

An unusual clause was written in the articles agreeing that 'all who sign for One Shilling per month shall be discharged as soon as the vessel is safely moored at the Quay at Sydney, cleaned and painted.' But this did not concern Conrad. It was the usual thing for smart passenger ships, wool-clippers and the like, to sign some additional crew for the outward run – stewards and an extra cook or two to look after the passengers, and six or ten ABs to build up the watches and help get a smart passage out of her. These other outward-bound shilling-a-monthers were passage workers, professional seamen who wanted to pay off legally in Australia and stay there, perhaps to try the gold-diggings for a while, more probably because they knew there was a considerable sea traffic out of Brisbane, Sydney, Melbourne and Hobart which offered seamen better pay, prospects and conditions than did most British ships, and the chance also to settle in the new country. There were usually a few qualified passage workers offering homewards, too, among those who found Australia not much to their liking or were just plain restless. These were welcome at the same rate of 'pay'. With sufficient watch-keeping strength, the master could hold his canvas longer and drive her harder, without undue risk of losing too many expensive sails.

But Conrad was a special case. He might have been considered an extra hand (for the articles declared twenty hands all told to be a sufficient crew) but he stayed aboard at Sydney, still on his shilling-a-month legal fiction – bound to the ship and working hard for her like everyone else. It appears that he was in fact required to sign off at Sydney, on 6 February 1879; but he signed on again at once. A second ordinary seaman by name E. J. Hartenstein, entered as of London, also did the round voyage for that nominal (and non-existent) shilling-a-month, and an Australian named Henry Horning, aged 17, joined for the round voyage Sydney – London – Sydney before the ship left Australia, on the same conditions.

The *Duke of Sutherland*'s arrival at Sydney is reported in the *Sydney Morning Herald* for 1 February 1879, along with the *Pacific*, schooner, from the Solomon Islands, another schooner from Queensland, and passenger steamers from Melbourne, Brisbane and Hobart Town. The ship brought a general cargo from London valued at £43,100 and the five passengers are named. She had left London on 15 October 1878, passed through the Downs two days later, and on 27 October was off Ushant in a heavy westerly gale, according to her report. She had no northeast trade winds, and crossed the Line on 30 November to find the southeast trade wind light and unfavourable. She passed the meridian of Good Hope on 26 December, 60 days out, and in making her easting only ordinary weather was experienced. The Southwest Cape of Tasmania was rounded on 20 January, and since then she had met only northeasterly winds. 'In 40N 20W a horned Owl, some Starlings and Larks, flew aboard, and were captured.'

In other words, Captain McKay is explaining away an indifferent passage. No trade winds, and poor westerlies too? Perhaps he had been inexpert at finding them. One of the sailing-ship master's essential skills was in finding wind – above all, in not running out of that essential force. Forty-six days to the Line, 26 thence to Good Hope, another month or more from there to Sydney through those splendid ship-chasers the Roaring Forties, to make 108 days in all? This sort of thing was all very well for the later-day wall-sided big 'windjammer', but was extremely slow for an alleged clipper. So the ship discharged her general cargo, and waited for wood and passengers to carry to England. There was no rush of either.

She was to wait at Sydney five months before filing for the homeward passage. Five months! That cost money – for berthing and other dues, advertising, everything her now reduced crew consumed. The 'shilling-a-monthers' (less Conrad) had gone, followed quickly by a couple of deserters and a seaman to hospital, reducing the 26 outwards crew to ten. They had been the usual cosmopolitan lot, including Canadians, a New Yorker, Swedes, Norwegians, Heligolanders, Irish and Germans, and a black man whose name appears as S. White – in fact it is recorded simply as X, for AB White or Wait or whoever he was could not write and someone else wrote in the name. He is entered as a Barbadian, from the ship *Boyne*.

However, Conrad had clearly been the most unusual member of the crew, for the official superintending the signing-on had taken the trouble to enter in red ink the official number of the honest little *Skimmer of the Sea*, as if he did not believe either in her or in Conrad's connection with the vessel: everyone else's last ship is accepted without any such verification.

Now and again, lest she be forgotten, her master and agent put optimistic announcements on the front page of the *Sydney Morning Herald* that the 'well-known Clipper Ship *Duke of Sutherland* 1,047 tons, will have quick dispatch.' Many other magnificent clipper ships and the occasional barque advertised similarly, mainly for wool and passengers. But no-one offered the *Duke* any high-quality wool: no-one applied for passage. March, April, May passed. Other ships sailed but the *Duke* seemed to be a fixture. No matter: the rest of the world was far away and the meals – not so bad in port – were regular; and whilst the ship was awaiting cargo and his name was on the articles, this counted as sea-time, essential for the would-be ship's officer. Conrad could make good use of his free time. His duties would not have been very onerous; they included acting as night watchman sometimes, which he enjoyed. In the afternoons he could walk up to the library, or stroll round to see the ships if he wished. Wherever he went the shapely masts and spars of clippers, real and alleged, reached for the sky.

It was July 1879 before the *Sydney Morning Herald* announced the sailing of the *Duke of Sutherland*, 1,140 tons (up a little) for London, with one passenger (and the Master's wife Mrs McKay) and an assorted cargo which included 285 bales of wool. She had lots of other stuff, a regular general cargo of it – 5,817 hides, 1,053 casks tallow, 3,230 cakes copper, 1 bale hair (human?), 239 tons shale, 7 bales waste, 450 cases meats, 18 bales horns, 40 bags hoofs, 108 bags bones, 12,870 treenails, 21 bales leather, 13 cases wine, 6 packages, and 'a quantity of glue pieces and assorted bones'. It was 5 July when she put to sea from anchorage for her wintry run towards Cape Horn.

Less than 300 bales of wool in five months! The few bales she managed to book were indifferent stuff of the kind that had its own market but brokers did not bid for at auctions. That word 'clipper' was much misused and still is, but if anyone knew the merits of ships claiming the title it was those who worked in Sydney's wool trade. It was very obvious that ships advertising an ability to catch such-and-such a wool auction in London must be relied upon to do so: it is equally obvious that nobody accepted the *Sutherland*'s claim at all. Indeed, she had given up making it long before she sailed, for as the weeks passed there was not an auction scheduled that year that she could catch, even if she ran home in 60 days.

In fact, when at last she sailed through Port Jackson's Heads on 6 July 1879 she took 106 days to reach London, and she did not return to Australia at all. She probably lost money on Conrad's voyage; for the owner is changed before the next – a tramping run round the Horn with South Welsh coal to Coquimbo in Chile, thence back with ore. The master is William Jones of Wales, who did not do very well, for he put into Rio de Janeiro on the outward passage and took another 78 days from Rio to Coquimbo (that should have been sufficient for the whole passage). She lost a fifteen-year-old out of her rigging off the Horn homewards. The next voyage she drove ashore at Timaru on the coast of New Zealand and became a total loss, as Conrad later regretfully acknowledged. This was in May 1882; nobody was calling her a 'clipper' then.

One gets an unexpected glimpse of the earnest young Pole in the *Sutherland*'s half-deck at that time from a letter that Alan Villiers found among the Basil Lubbock papers at the National Maritime Museum at Greenwich. The letter was written by the young Sydney man Henry Horning, dated 20 April 1930 – 50 years after the voyage, but his memories were vivid. The young Horning had worked his passage – a round voyage, actually – at the 'wage' of one shilling a month, too, living in the half-deck. It appears that Horning Senior was a friend of Captain McKay: hence the son's voyage. According to Horning, Conrad

> occupied one of the top bunks (in the half-deck) and I the lower. He was a Pole of dark complexion, (and) black hair ... In his watches below, he spent all his time reading and writing English: he spoke with a foreign accent. I can well remember his favourite habit of sitting in his bunk with his legs dangling over the side (of a low bunk-board) and either a book or writing material on his lap. How he came to occupy a bunk in the half-deck instead of one in the t'gallant forecastle is beyond me.

Young Horning's worldly experience must have been slight at the time or he would have understood well enough that Conrad occupied 'privileged' quarters for the same reason as Horning – that he did not belong in ship's forecastles.

The *Duke of Sutherland* ran her easting down and was off the Horn in winter, with both Conrad and Horning aboard. She was bound east – the 'downhill' way to old sailors – but the experience could scarcely have been pleasant. There can be a lot of easterly wind down there in winter and, when the wind has any south in it, it is savagely cold. Nothing ever invented was windier and more exposed than a square-rigger's masts and yards, and the *Duke of Sutherland* also had an open wheel, as was the British style – an unprotected wheel exposed on the open poop, and two-hour turns at handling it. This was the limejuicer's 'style', for it was considered proper for the helmsman to be exposed to all weather. It was proper, indeed (for he got better 'feel' of the stumbling ship that way), but not so as to die from it, or feel that death could be a merciful relief.

Tough as the homeward-bound passage of the *Duke of Sutherland* may have been, it was invaluable experience for Conrad. It completed his four years' sea-time: but, much more importantly, it enabled him to learn a great deal more about sailing ships. Merely to live a year in such a ship and in such a trade was to absorb matters of practical seamanship by the book-full, and Conrad was obviously most observant and gifted with an excellent memory. What he had to do now was to marshal his knowledge and study at least one of the several volumes available of seamanship 'questions and answers' prepared for those about to present themselves for inquisition before the Board of Trade's examiners.

Unfortunately, the standard works in this field were extremely dull and some were difficult, for what they largely contrived to do was to put into lifeless prose all sorts of sail-handling and ship-handling difficulties, which would have become second nature to the candidate in question but could be confusing and complicated when some elderly, cold-eyed examiner called upon him, in a bare and hostile room, to narrate in clear prose just how he would tack a full-rigged ship, or wear her, or – a favourite which happened only in Board of Trade examinations – club-haul her off a lee shore that suddenly loomed up out of fog. That fog was apt to spread rapidly into the candidate's mind, and his description become limping and inarticulate: for what many of those examiners could require to be done with a poor ship was often highly imaginative, always instantly demanding, and sometimes almost impossible. Poor Conrad! And all in the third language he had had to master in a short and sometimes eventful lifetime in which he had done well to survive at all.

But he did not hurry to that execution-block, his first Board of Trade examination.

Loch Etive

Conrad completed his necessary sea-time of four years by serving as an ordinary seaman on the tramp steamer *Europa*, from 12 December 1879 to the end of January 1880. There appear to be no official papers extant for this vessel, although she could have been a London steamer of 666 tons, built at Newcastle in 1862, which was in the Mediterranean trade in the 1870s. It appears from the Bobrowski correspondence that Conrad quarrelled with her master, a Captain Munro, about money. In any case, he signed off, took lodgings, and submitted himself for examination as second mate.

Conrad must have found the examination a profound ordeal. In *A Personal Record*, he states that his examiner (who was a Captain James Rankin),

> must, I am forced to conclude, have been unfavourably impressed by something in my appearance. His old thick hands, loosely clasped, resting on his crossed legs, he began an elementary question in a mild voice, and went on, went on ... It lasted for hours. (*A Personal Record*, page 113)

When Conrad was eventually released, the clerk commented that he had been kept for just under three hours, and that he had never known so long an examination.

However, it is reasonable to suppose that it was not Conrad's appearance that impressed his examiner unfavourably, but his application form, which contained his record of sea-time. This certificate still exists, and reads as follows:

Ship's name	Rig	Port of Registry	Rank	Years	Months	Days
Mont Blanc	Bark	Marseilles	Midshipman	1		
St Antoine	Bark	Marseilles	3rd Mate	2		13
Duke of Sutherland	Ship	Wick	O.S.		11	25
Europa	Str.	London	A.B		2	18
Total service at sea				4	2	26
Total for which certificates produced				4	1	22

The sequence of ranks is bizarre, and may even have caused Conrad's record as a whole to seem fraudulent. Midshipmen do not immediately become third mates, nor revert thereafter to ordinary seaman. Captain Rankin must have been very puzzled by all this, and must have taken the time to assure himself that this most unusual candidate really had served his sea-time, especially in the French ships he claimed. In fact, there is a line scored right through that bold claim of two years and thirteen days for the very inexperienced alleged third mate of the barque *Saint Antoine*.

However, Captain Rankin must have been favourably impressed by Conrad, and he must have decided that, whatever his real capacity had been in the *Mont Blanc* and *Saint Antoine*, he was now a competent and experienced seaman, fit for charge of a watch at sea. He passed.

It was a splendid achievement, and one about which Conrad's uncle was enthusiastic and congratulatory. He wrote to his nephew saying that 'You have given me real pleasure and my first reward.' It was a major achievement: not only that Conrad should have overcome so many difficulties, but also that the Board of Trade should have perceived and recognised the qualities of so unusual a candidate.

Now, once again, he needed a ship.

That hard-won second mate's certificate was a triumph; but it brought no job with it. Conrad would have felt both elated and depressed: feelings he put into the mouth of his young narrator in the novel *Chance*, written in 1913.

> I found myself downstairs without being aware of the steps as if I had floated down the staircase. The finest day in my life. The day you get your first command is nothing to it ... What comes after is about the most unpleasant time for a youngster, the trying to get an officer's berth with nothing to show but a brand-new certificate. It is surprising how useless you find that piece of ass's skin that you have been putting yourself in such a state about. (*Chance*, chapter 1)

What could the newly qualified ship's officer do to obtain a berth? There were many sailing-ship lines then based in London, but without influence, he was unlikely to be considered for any vacancy that might arise. Tadeusz Bobrowski had been lucky or clever enough to know influential people in Marseille, but he had no such connections in London. Shipping lines very naturally fostered their own men, brought along in the company in question as apprentices, reported on by the company's own masters, and selected for any vacancy that might arise in automatic preference to an outsider. Any spare third or second officers' positions would be reserved for them, if possible. The new officer filled in forms, but never got past the office boys in his vain quest for a post. It was all rather difficult, and could be expensive: doing nothing usually is. Conrad would have been grateful for the continuing allowance from his kind uncle Tadeusz, for otherwise he might soon have gone hungry. At least he had a roof over his head at his lodgings at 6 Dynevor Road, Stoke Newington – the address he used on official forms for a number of years, after his first voyage to Sydney.

There *was* one unorthodox way to get to sea. This was known as the pier-head jump. It happened all too often in those wild old days that after a new crew had been signed on ashore in the proper manner a day or so before the outward-bounder moved from her berth, one or two might not join, or join and disappear again, or somehow be absent when the tide served and she had to lock out and begin the voyage. Or a man might be taken ill at the last moment and have to be landed. It was more or less customary for an out-of-work seaman or two to be about in the right place – by the lock-gates or near the pier-head – as ships locked out, with a 'donkey's breakfast' (straw mattress) and his sea-bag, his papers in his pocket, ready to leap (literally) into the breach, sign the articles forthwith, and off to sea. This was the 'pier-head jump'. But it was very rare for a watch-keeping officer to be replaced in that hurried manner.

It *could* happen; but possible replacement officers did not hang about the pier-heads for such a rare chance. Ships suddenly bereft of an officer through emergency had to take other action, and that was to get in touch quickly with their agents, or the Shipping Office, or some authority who might know of an officer with the proper qualifications who could make himself instantly available. Among the officials and other contacts Conrad called on regularly was such a man. So when the *Loch Etive* of the Scots 'Loch' line found herself short of a second mate just as she had to slip from her berth, tow to the dock entrance, and lock out, on a bright morning in August 1880, it so happened that Conrad's friend found himself urgently appealed to for an instant replacement.

The deep-laden Loch liner was just about to sail direct for Sydney, Australia, with a full general cargo. The second officer of the *Loch Etive* had been knocked down by a restive dray-horse while he was hurrying through the dock-gate with the ship's clearance papers, and was too seriously injured to proceed on the voyage. Conrad used this episode in *Chance* as well, suitably changed. The master, Captain Anthony, interviews the new second mate who has been thrust upon him by chance:

> I suppose he had heard I was freshly passed and without experience as an officer, because he turned about and looked me over as if I had been exposed for sale.
>
> 'He's young', he muttered. 'Looks smart, though … You're smart and willing (this to me very sudden and loud) and all that, aren't you?'
>
> I just managed to open and shut my mouth, no more, being taken unawares. But it was enough for him. He made is if I had deafened him with protestations of my smartness and willingness. (*Chance*, chapter 1)

What Captain Stuart of the *Loch Etive* thought when he met his new third mate is not recorded. As to his inexperience, this was not crucial. Captain Stuart promoted his third mate to second and made Conrad his new third mate. Third mate was a dogsbody's job, for the chief and second mates were the watch-keepers and an excellent old Clydeside bos'n ran the hands. This left the third as spare watch-keeper, useful in emergency, a stand-in for meal reliefs, at the beck and call of the mate (as the chief was always known), on deck with him in bad weather, and acting as 'dayman' in good. But he would never get the chance to be in charge of a watch himself. Many ships would make a senior apprentice acting third mate, and excellent officers they often were. Perhaps the Loch line had a company rule against this.

The Glasgow Lochs were known as smart clippers, but the *Loch Etive* was a newer version with rather fuller lines, forced upon her owners to permit the stowage of more and perhaps bulkier cargo on her 'general-out, wool-home' round, to earn more and still make fast passages to catch the wool auctions (which she did, invariably). Indeed she was still a clipper, unlike the *Duke of Sutherland*, though she never made anything like a passage to compare with the 69 days Sydney to London by the *Tweed*, Captain Stuart's previous ship, in 1875–76.

This was Captain Stuart's not-so-secret grief. His previous ship was one of the 'cracks', and the *Loch Etive* could never touch her good performances. The *Tweed* was an odd ship, something of a freak, or perhaps a 'fluke', as she began her career designed as a steamship. As such, in those days, she needed a hull that would slip easily through the water and give her the essential endurance to make long ocean passages, since steamers had to be able to travel considerable distances between refuelling. By God's grace and the love of good shipwrights, she never had one of those abrupt, up-and-down graceless steamship bows, for even steamers were designed as ships then. This paid under sail, too, though the other Loch liners had the greater capacity (and, consequently, the poorer speed). That old steamer, converted to engineless full-rigged ship, skipped along happily all the rest of her life as if overjoyed at the removal of the noisy engine, stokehold (coal) and boilers, and the vibration, smuts and noise that went with those unnecessary things.

Captain Stuart was obviously a kindred spirit, and danced her round the world at a speed that delighted both of them – and would have greatly pleased Conrad too. How pleasant was her clean wake, her stately advance in gracious silence, sung to only by the wind and the lilt of the sprays at the curve of her cutwater.

The *Tweed* was built as the auxiliary frigate *Punjaub* in India in 1857, for the Honourable East India Company. Later on, converted to a cargo-carrying sailing ship without power, she belonged to John Willis, who is said to have used her lines very largely for the design of his *Cutty Sark*. Willis renamed her the *Tweed*. Those who had known Captain Stuart as master of the *Tweed* understood well enough why, when master of the *Loch Etive*, he showed little sign of affection for the new ship and drove her relentlessly. Certainly the driving was to some purpose, for no-one had ever questioned the *Loch Etive*'s right to load at one of Sydney's clipper berths for the London sales. She may not have been as fast as the *Tweed*, but she was a fine ship – a liner in a line trade, no parish-rigged old tramp, staggering slovenly about the hostile sea beyond her time.

When Conrad joined the laden ship was locking out, bound down-Thames, past Kent, down-channel, and to sea upon that long, hard road that led ships to Sydney, New South Wales. Not so much led them, perhaps, as permitted their passage when hard-driven, day and night, week-in, week-out, for anything from 75 days (if very fortunate) to 105 if not. That good fortune must include large areas of steady and fresh trade winds; a thin doldrums belt and tractable 'horse latitudes'; and a quick passage through the wild west winds from wind'ard of Tristan da Cunha, past Good Hope and along that road of savage sea and snarling squalls and sleet and icebergs and unlit islands that stretched between there and Australia – 6,000 miles just of that!

The *Loch Etive* arrived in Sydney without incident, and was back in London by April 1881. She was obviously a splendid ship, and competently run by a first-class master – a very good experience for Conrad in his first voyage abaft the mast in a British ship. He was a fortunate young man to have been a junior officer in a Loch liner, even though the experience was of no direct help in his professional advancement. Before he could present himself for examination for his chief mate's certificate he had to be able to prove that he had served a full year at least as a watch-keeping officer in charge of a watch in a deepwater square-rigged ship. He had in fact been allowed to stand a proper watch on that round voyage only for a few days, when the second mate was ill, and this would not count at all. He needed a solid spell as a watch-keeping second mate in his own right, to build on the useful experience of the *Loch Etive*, and to further his chosen career in sail in the approved and necessary manner.

That Danish brig

In the fine sketch 'Initiation' in *The Mirror of the Sea* (which is subtitled *Memories and Impressions*) Conrad writes a vivid and dramatic account of rescuing the crew of a sinking Danish brig in the North Atlantic (pages 137–148). It has been suggested by knowledgeable seamen that if this account is based, at least in origin, on a personal experience of the author, then it must have occurred when he was third mate of the *Loch Etive*. There is a clue to this in that Conrad speaks of himself as having taken command of one of the boats of a ship 'famous for never losing steerage way as long as there was air enough to float a feather' (page 139) and picking off the nine-man crew of the brig almost as the falsely placid sea gurgled across her decks for the last time, and closed over her for ever. The *Loch Etive* would have fitted the description of sailing well in light winds more exactly than the other ships in which Conrad served. Moreover, he was a junior officer in the *Loch*, and in his account of a marine rescue; and Captain Stuart of the *Loch Etive* fits the character of the master of the rescue ship: impatient and sarcastic, but a good seaman. Finally, Conrad writes in *The Mirror of the Sea* (published in 1906) that the episode occurred 25 years previously, i.e. in 1881, when he was on the *Loch Etive*.

The description of the actual rescue is quietly and movingly told. Two of the ship's boats had launched together and raced for the brig, which was on the point of sinking:

> It was a very good race. At the finish there was not an oar's length between the first and second boat, with Death coming in a good third on the top of the very next smooth swell, for all one knew to the contrary …
>
> It had been a weirdly silent rescue – a rescue without a hail, without a single uttered word … Up to the very last moment those on board stuck to their pumps, which spouted two clear streams of water upon their bare feet … the two small bunches of half-naked, tattered men went on bowing from the waist to each other in their back-breaking labour, up and down, absorbed, with no time for a glance over the shoulder at the help that was coming to them. (*Mirror of the Sea*, page 141)

But nine imperilled seamen cannot be plucked from the sea and established in a British ship without at least some token glance towards officialdom. Although the loss of small wooden sailing vessels in the North Atlantic was then common, the arrival in the Thames of the *Loch Etive* with the master and eight other survivors from such a wreck would not go unnoticed. But there is no mention in the surviving papers from the ship of any such rescue, nor does a diligent search of the daily and shipping papers at the time of her arrival discover mention of any such incident as having anything to do with her.

Nor could it have happened during Conrad's previous voyage in the *Duke of Sutherland*, for he was an ordinary seaman in that ship and not third mate, and the ship's papers are equally silent; nor did Conrad's shipmate Horning, who was an apprentice aboard and wrote an account of his experience afloat, make any reference to any such incident.

Searches for a clue on the part of experts such as Captain P. A. MacDonald (of the ship *Dunsyre* and many more) have yielded nothing directly. Sunken ships, drifting derelicts, now and again a piece of quiet heroism to relieve the tragedies – yes, all these in plenty. But there is nothing to connect personally with the *Loch Etive* or Conrad and his actual seafaring.

It might have happened in one of his ships when homeward-bound – the *Narcissus* in 1884, for example, or the *Tilkhurst* when she returned to home waters without her injured mate in 1885, although hardly in the *Torrens* when he was mate. As a well-known passenger carrier, that ship would have been in the news if her people had made any such rescue. Both the *Narcissus* and the *Tilkhurst* made wide swings through the northern waters of the North Atlantic, as all homeward-bound square-riggers were forced to do by the very nature of the northeast trade winds. They made part of the homeward passage on or close to the normal east-bound trans-Atlantic route for ships bound for the English Channel. There is no mention of a sinking Danish brig, or any such incident, neither in the daily press nor in any of these ships' own logs and papers.

There was, however, one brief news item published in the shipping news of the *Sydney Morning Herald* of 2 April 1879, when Conrad was night-watchman on the *Duke of Sutherland*, which could be relevant. 'Terrible Sufferings at Sea', the small headline runs above the account of the rescue by the Danish steamer *Harald* of the crew of an English schooner *Able Seaman* from New Brunswick, on 40 degrees north 60 degrees west,

> in a helpless state, threatening to go to the bottom at any moment, the waves constantly breaking over the deck which was swept quite clear. Two men being observed on the after-deck, the Mate of the *Harald* and four sailors at once volunteered to attempt to save the crew. A boat was launched. Five more men were seen huddled on the deck. With great effort, all seven men were got in the boat, half-dead from exposure and hunger and nearly blind, with their hands suffering from mortification. During five days they had not tasted food or water and they were unable to account at all for the last two days, for they had given up all hope of being saved ... The poor fellows received every assistance aboard the *Harald*, and were safely landed at Antwerp.

Such incidents, the sighting of wooden derelicts large and small – usually small – were a common North Atlantic experience, and indeed hazard, and *Lloyd's Shipping Intelligence* ran a column of them in almost every issue (and still did so when Alan Villiers was sailing the ship *Joseph Conrad* in 1934–36). The US Hydrographic Office pilot charts plotted them and tried to show their drifting tacks, for a derelict ship, awash and all but invisible in breaking seas at night, was a terrible menace to steamers running into them at speed. Timber cargoes kept many afloat, and warships and US Coast Guard cutters were sent to search for and sink them if they could.

It seems reasonably safe to conclude that the rescue described so well in *The Mirror of the Sea* did not derive from any experience undergone by Conrad as a junior officer in the *Loch Etive*. Where it did come from is unclear. It may have been based on an incident on another ship, of which we have no record; from a seaman's yarn in port; or from an account of a maritime disaster of which he read in the press. We know that Conrad had plenty of experience of pumping for life himself, as second mate in the sea-thirsty little barque *Palestine*. She did her best to sink several times, and all hands had to man the pumps continuously and for long hours. This could certainly have given Conrad part of the background he used so effectively in his account of the sinking of the Danish brig.

Conrad may have invented this dramatic episode to illustrate the moment 'I had become a seaman at last' – because he saw 'the duplicity of the sea's most tender mood' (*Mirror of the Sea*, pages 141–142). But he heartily disliked too close an attention being paid to the origins of his writings. He wrote to an inquirer:

> It is a strange fate that everything I have, of set artistic purpose, laboured to leave indefinite, suggestive, in the penumbra of initial inspiration, should have that light turned on it and its insignificance (as compared with, I might say without megalomania, the ampleness of my conceptions) for any fool to comment upon or even for average minds to be disappointed with.[3]

We stand rebuked. In this book we try to steer a clear course away from the reefs and shallows of 'identifying' Conrad's fictional ships, characters and places, and towards the fairer winds and safer waters of his actual career in the merchant service, in which an informed and deliberate interest is legitimate. But the sirens of speculation have always been tempting.

---

3. Richard Curle (ed.), *Conrad to a Friend: 150 Selected Letters from Joseph Conrad to Richard Curle.* Sampson Low, Marston & Co., London, 1928.

Palestine

Conrad next appears to have been mixed up with a full-rigged ship named the *Anna* or *Annie Frost*, but this is the vaguest ship and the vaguest episode in his entire marine career. For years, this mysterious vessel eluded the most industrious of marine researchers, delving back through the shipping records to check on details of the Polish author's career at sea: an investigation he would not have helped, but would perhaps have treated with a faint irony. Was there ever such a ship as the *Anna Frost*, and if so, did Conrad sail in her?

Not for the first time, Conrad's correspondence with his uncle in the Ukraine sheds some light on this episode, but does not entirely clarify it. From the Bobrowski letters it appears that his nephew had represented to his uncle that he had shipped in the *Anna Frost* for a long voyage.[4] The ship had foundered. Conrad survived but lost his gear, and sought an extra £10 to cover its replacement. (Such a sum would not have covered his requirements for oilskins, bedding, hard weather and tropical clothing, even in the 1880s.)

A Canadian wooden ship of 1,236 tons, built in Quebec in 1863 and named the *Annie Frost*, was still listed in Lloyd's Register of Shipping for 1869. She sailed from the Port of London for Cochin China (now Vietnam) on 31 July 1881, or cleared outwards on that day. According to the search made by Captain P. A. McDonald (a friend and colleague of Alan Villiers), this ship sank in the North Atlantic in 1882 when outward bound towards India. There was no J. Conrad or J. Korzeniowski on her articles then, or any trace that he had been in the ship. This, however, cannot be taken as proof that he had never served on board: for he may have been a 'runner'.

The custom was that, to save costs, a deepwater sailing ship paid off her deep-sea crew as soon as possible after reaching her port of discharge. These dispersed as with the sea winds and never reassembled. Shore workers discharged the cargo and put in a little replacement ballast (for few ships could be trusted to stand up empty, even in the quietest dock). In due course, the ship would be chartered for a further long voyage, but she would have to go first to the outward loading port. It was uneconomic to sail a full sailing crew for this, as many cargoes, such as coal, could require a long wait for their turn to load: hence the 'runners' came in. They were the minimum number of hands needed to look after the ship, then usually under tow, for passage to the loading port only. They kept her clean, steered, tended the tow-line, rigged out the jib-boom (if necessary) on arrival, and

---

4. Jocelyn Baines, *Joseph Conrad: a Critical Biography*. Weidenfeld & Nicolson, London, 1960.

looked after themselves. For this, they were paid an agreed lump sum, and the runners were usually good seamen temporarily out of a regular berth.

Conrad might have served in a run crew while he was ashore from the *Loch Etive*. If it were on the *Anna Frost*, she was reported as striking the dock-gates at Le Havre and suffering some minor damage when setting out from that French port in tow towards London (which would presumably have been the loading port). The run had to be put off, and the runners were temporarily stranded. In such straits, £10 from any source would be welcome.

The young Pole next turned up in the oddest old vessel that even he ever found. With square-rigged ships available by the thousand, beautiful iron vessels coming from the splendid Clydeside and other shipyards in a final flowering of sea-kindly magnificence, at least a score of real clippers still racing across the seas, and sailing ships still in the passenger trade (but not many there) and dominating the tramp-cargo trades to the Far East, the west coast of the Americas and all Australasia, Second Mate J. Konrad Korzeniowski found an utterly insignificant little barque named *Palestine* lying in a dark pool in one of the smaller London docks, a pigeon among the eagles, a duckling among the swans – laid up, silent, apparently abandoned, with what looked like the dust of ages assembled on her minute decks.

Conrad, using the *Palestine* in a story called *Youth*, changed her name to the *Judea* and described her as 'all rust, dust, grime; soot aloft, dirt on deck.' The *Palestine* would certainly have looked so to a young sailor just off a smart Loch liner.

Although built in 1857 – the year Conrad was born in the Ukraine – the *Palestine* was not old for a well-built British wooden ship. Indeed, she should just have been entering the prime of life. A few weeks left crewless in the Shadwell basin would soon make her appear grimy; but this was superficial, and Conrad had an eye for outcasts such as this. The *Palestine*, for all her grime and London dirt of the moment, was a thoroughly shapely, graceful little vessel, symmetrical of rig and sweet in form – the sort to catch the eye of a poet. She had atmosphere, and Conrad was responsive to that.

She was by no means an undersized version of a larger barque, but an expression of the perfection of development of their own day – the 1850s – and the discerning eye of the true seaman could see this. She was no discarded runt among the big full-riggers and four-masted barques, either; rather were some of them overgrown, fattened versions of her, their hulls bloated to store some thousands of tons more cargo aboard, sacrificing grace and line and true sea-kindliness in the process.

The *Palestine* needed a second mate. (Little ships like her had no use for a third.) The master was an elderly man who had a share in her. He was a seaman of the old school, the gnarled, hand-sewn type with stout-fingered, competent hands, a man brought up on Geordie ships on the tough North Sea, who'd heard the sound of the wind in the rigging from his cradle – a type of man now quite vanished from a heedless earth that probably never deserved him.

The *Palestine* would soon be sailing up the North Sea bound for North Shields to load a full cargo of coal for Bangkok, in the country then known as Siam. The second mate's wage was four pounds a month. That wage was a pound below the rate ruling in the port for deep-sea sailing-ship second mates, and in fact below the wage of the ship's carpenter. No matter. Conrad signed. The second mate's cabin was small but adequate, like the barque herself, and it looked as if it would keep most of the sea out. In any case, the voyage from the United Kingdom to Bangkok would be something of a flying-fish passage, once they were across the Bay of Biscay.

The new articles were signed on 19 September 1881 in London, and still exist within the keeping of the Public Records Office of that city, once the largest and busiest port in the world. (The *Palestine* was an exceptionally well-documented ship, and her history previous to her loss is recorded in great detail in her official logs. Some details are included here in the appendix, as they give a unique and vivid picture of what life could be like on a small passenger-carrying sailing ship.)

Conrad appears on the articles as Konrad Korzeniowski, aged 24, of Gittomir, Poland. His last ship is given as the *Loch Ettif*, which must have been his pronunciation. The mate is an elderly gentleman named Mahon, who is to be paid six pounds a month. The crew of thirteen all told was small but thoroughly international, including some Norwegians, a Canadian, a Hollander, a Newfoundlander and a Finn. However, none of these was to make the voyage, for the *Palestine* was to change her crew several times before she finally left coastal waters for Bangkok.

Within a day or two of Conrad's signing, the barque slipped from the dock and made her way under easy sail down the Thames. It was the time of the autumnal equinox – a bad time for elderly (or should we say mature?) barques to be in the North Sea. The equinoctial gales howled, and the *Palestine* sheltered off Gravesend for almost a week, and was then the best part of a month reaching her loading port in North Shields. (Whether or not Conrad reflected on the progress he had made since serving as an ordinary seaman on the *Skimmer of the Sea* is not recorded.)

This meant that the *Palestine* lost her turn for a berth to coal, and was lucky not to lose her charter altogether. This seemed to bother her elderly master not at all, and her second mate even less. What he then needed most was twelve months' certificated service as a regular watch-keeping officer in a deep-sea vessel, and the *Palestine's* round voyage to Bangkok should just about provide that. Moreover, time waiting for a cargo counted towards sea-time. However, such were the delays of the good ship *Palestine* that it began to look as if Conrad would manage his certified year without leaving English waters.

The shapely little barque was damaged in the dock when a floundering box of an empty tramp steamer bashed into her, having been taken charge of by the wind. The *Palestine* was not damaged seriously. Her hull was still sound, and her rigging intact, but it imposed another delay on what was already proving a very slow start for Bangkok, as the damage had to be assessed and repairs made.

It was almost the end of November 1881 before the *Palestine* slipped quietly seawards from the Tyne with 557 tons of best West Hartlepool coal under hatches, bound directly on the long road towards Bangkok. She would sail down the North Sea, then through the English Channel, with the possibility of being compelled to turn and take on the rougher road around the north of Scotland, if persistent hard southwesterlies made the shorter route impossible.

All this was just the beginning, the road to sea-room. Then came the length of both North and South Atlantics, the trade winds helping in part, although the southeast trade might push her towards the coast of Brazil, which many a sailing ship had grazed in error – or remained where she struck, for the land may be as unkind to the ship as the sea. The *Palestine* would then make her easting to run in the Roaring Forties around the Cape of Good Hope at the bottom of Africa, and make more longitude until it was time to turn northwards towards Krakatoa and the narrow straits between Sumatra and Java.

Next came the Java Sea, part of the South China Sea, and finally the full length of the Gulf of Siam, with a litter of reef-fringed isles and islets to avoid from the Sunda Straits onwards. All this was to be accomplished only by the wind and the master's use of it, under God.

It reads like a saga. It was in fact a commonplace passage of the sort that the little *Palestine* had successfully accomplished on at least twenty previous voyages to Australia, China, Singapore, Ceylon (now Sri Lanka), Saigon and the Philippines, at first often with passengers. She carried less than six hundred tons of cargo and many of her voyages took three to five months, and sometimes more.

That so small a ship could be usefully employed on such long hauls seems now strange to the point of being incomprehensible. The essence of the matter, however, was that she had only to earn an appreciable amount more than her costs, and these were very low. The *Palestine* was manned by a regular crew of fourteen. If she carried passengers, this might become seventeen or eighteen, but it was still a very low total. A few passengers might be carried aft, and be treated in comparative comfort, messing with the ship's officers. Usually, however, most passengers travelled rough in makeshift accommodation fitted temporarily in the hold. They did their own stewarding, and easily paid their way.

The entire watch-keeping afterguard consisted of mate and bos'n, under the master, and the steward doubled as cook. Even those doubled duties were not onerous, although he also baked the bread, if any, and looked after the stock: maybe a hog or two and a few chickens. All else was salted, smoked or fried. The wages bill was small. Able seamen cost two pounds and ten shillings or three pounds a month, and ordinary seamen half that: and of course apprentices cost nothing but their keep, and might even contribute towards that. The daily cost of food ran at most to seven or eight pence a seaman. Small sailing ships served remote ports with few facilities or dues. As a general rule, crews worked their own cargoes in and out at anchorage themselves, at no extra payment. If fresh food was not cheaper than the ship's provisions, it was not bought. Tugs were not hired: small sailing ships used their own sails, or tided or kedged themselves in and out of harbour, or even towed themselves with their own ship's boat. Since capital costs were low, so were insurance and depreciation. Since the owner might also be master, management overheads did not exist: and nor was there a need for cablegrams, communications or vacations.

The earliest articles of the *Palestine* still surviving relate to a passage to Egypt in 1859 when she set sail with a crew of fourteen, including the master. The crew contained three apprentices, three ordinary seamen, who were in effect still boys, and a stiffening of four able seamen, two in each watch. Some of the last great sailing ships began voyages with similarly tiny numbers.

So the economics of ships such as the *Palestine* (and the *Skimmer of the Sea* before she became a coastal collier) become understandable. There were at least a dozen such small ships knocking about the Tasman Sea and the nearer South Sea islands when Alan Villiers was a boy in Melbourne before the First World War. There were old-timers like the barque *Wild Wave* (258 tons, built of wood in Liverpool in 1875) and the iron barque *Manurewa* (371 tons, built as the *Vale Royal* at Port Glasgow in 1884), as well as three-masted barquentines and other small traders that were still earning their keep in the 1920s.

The *Palestine* staggered reluctantly down the North Sea with a full cargo of coal in some very stormy weather, and did not seem at all fond of the prospect of the lengthy voyage ahead of her. At the Channel she baulked altogether. She opened up when a succession of gales smacked at her and kept on screaming in her rigging as if they hated her. After less than a month at sea, and having sailed no more than two or three hundred miles on her journey from England to Bangkok, she was leaking badly. Captain Beard was forced to turn, and she did well to limp back half-awash to Falmouth, traditionally not only a port where ships reported for orders but where they went for repairs, and in any case his nearest viable English port. Her serious leak, caused by the straining of the hull full of coal being forever flung about in the stormy waters of the North Sea, began on Christmas Eve.

Christmas Eve! There was no good time for a ship to spring a leak, but the eve of the birth of Christ was an especially mean occasion for the sea to break in, and with the ship still having made such little progress. It was pump or swim, and the tossing grey waters looked very cold and nasty for swimming. They pumped, and went on pumping.

This is how Conrad described it in *Youth*, a story based very largely on his experiences in the *Palestine*:

> And we pumped. And there was no break in the weather. The sea was white like a sheet of foam, like a cauldron of boiling milk: there was not a break in the clouds, no – not the size of a man's hand – no, not for so much as ten seconds. There was for us no stay, there were for us no stars, no sun, no universe – nothing but angry clouds and an infuriated sea. We pumped watch and watch for dear life ... we had forgotten how it felt to be dry.

It took over two weeks to stagger back to Falmouth, pumping all the time – that spirit-sapping, dreadful work. The ship found safe anchorage in the River Fal on 10 January 1882, and all hands thanked God, still pumping, although the hull tightened somewhat when the strain of pitching, yawing and rolling in the Channel seas departed in the sheltered

Palestine afire in Bangka Strait

Riversdale running into an anchorage

Narcissus running up-Channel

Tilkhurst discharging cargo at Calcutta

water. Perhaps the leak was not so serious. Some of the crew did not wait to find out, but promptly deserted. This was the only course open to them if they wished to leave the ship, for they were not then entitled to be paid off. They had signed on to make the voyage, and that voyage they were legally bound to make – or quietly disappear during the night without the pittance that was their due.

The remainder discharged some coal, found a leak or two in the topsides, fixed these, and sailed again, for optimism may be restored for a while in quiet waters. This optimism was unwarranted. Outside, the long-suffering *Palestine* opened up once again, worse than ever. This time she did not sail far, but hurried back to Falmouth, where the shipwrights may not have been entirely unsurprised to see her.

Now all the coal, except for some 70 or 80 tons which it was essential to retain as ballast, was hoisted out of the hold, and the barque was slipped. Large amounts of oakum had wept out of her seams under the battering of the sea, and had to be skilfully hammered in again. The work was slow, noisy and time-consuming, and like the oakum, the crew began to seep away.

A month later, the *Palestine* was still there. By now she had become a fixture in the harbour and a feature of the town, to be pointed out to curious visitors. There she lay, the little *Palestine*, whom the sea had tried to drown twice. Destination: Bangkok. Cargo: coal, now lying on the jetty. Crew: missing. Date of departure: uncertain. The *Palestine* in fact remained in Falmouth for so long that before she set out for Bangkok once more, the second mate had gained almost all the sea-time he needed to sit for his next certificate, counting from the barque's departure from the Thames. She had been a sea-going ship ever since, at least in the records of officialdom. In all that time, Conrad had served as a watch-keeping officer for about a month, but sea-time has been claimed more brazenly – a little, perhaps, even by himself.

Just why an ambitious and able, if such an unusual young man, telling himself that he was bent on a seafaring career, chose to remain in so lowly an ocean wanderer idle in port for so long, it is difficult to say. Uncle Tadeusz Bobrowski took a poor view of the *Palestine*'s inexhaustible thirst for sea water. That same uncle, one remembers, was under the impression that his unfortunate nephew had recently been wrecked in the *Anna Frost*, since that is precisely what his nephew had told him. Now his wayward ward seemed determined to have a wooden ship founder under him! Another berth as second mate, in a ship that actually went to sea rather than making the sea part of its cargo, was surely not that difficult to find.

But the *Palestine* held the young Korzeniowski in thrall, lowly little barque though she was. She had an attraction that both the *Duke of Sutherland* and *Loch Etive* had lacked, fine full-riggers as they may have been. Perhaps it was a human afterguard. Captain Beard was a fine old man, although his qualities as a master had long been overlooked, since this was his first command: too late in a hard life, perhaps. What had held him back before? He was a gentle man, a quietly memorable man; and his little barque had the same qualities.

Perhaps he had taken a long time and made many efforts to pass for his master's certificate. It was not unknown.

'His eyes were perfectly angelic,' his unusual second mate wrote of him years afterwards in a letter to his friend H. G. Wells, when both Wells and he were masters in another world. 'This is not a sentimental exaggeration, but an honest attempt to convey the truth.' In Falmouth, Captain Beard was a man past seventy, with no pension and few savings from a hard life. What he had was peace in those old blue eyes, and Conrad saw it. One may see the young Polish seaman, whose own father had died when he was eleven, continuing unquestioningly aboard the barque that such a man commanded, for the barque had peace too, and poetry in her, and atmosphere.

Conrad responded to such things. One notes it more than once in his choice of ship, before and after the doomed barque *Palestine*. The old *Skimmer* for one, even when reduced to coastwise coal-humping; the gracious little French vessels, including the *Tremolino*; the sweet-lined iron *Narcissus*; his only command, the *Otago*; and in the end the gracious old sailing-passenger-liner *Torrens*, a noble ship which, if past her prime when Conrad signed her articles, still knew her share of quiet glory.

The *Palestine* left Falmouth, sailed down both Atlantics, rounded the Cape of Good Hope, and made her longitude east. But she never reached Bangkok. Her cargo of best West Hartlepool coal, too long aboard and too often wet, caught fire when she turned the last corner: in the South China Sea, towards the Gulf of Siam. She had not leaked again, for the Falmouth shipwrights had done their work well. But coals are a dangerous cargo on very long hauls.

So serious was the risk of fire in coal cargoes, that the subject had been considered by a Royal Commission in 1875. Commenting on this, an article in the *Shipping Gazette Weekly Summary* of 14 April 1892 reported that 57 coal-laden sailing ships were known to have been lost because of their burning cargo and another 328, similarly laden, were missing. From 1879 to 1892, the loss/missing rate was 25 a year. Like the *Palestine*, they were comparatively small ships; but this is an appalling total. Speculation on the chief causes included theories about the action of iron pyrites on the coal in ships' holds, an absorption of oxygen by new coal which was said to amount to twice its own volume. Professor Lewes of the Royal Naval College at Dartmouth recommended the placing of steel bottles of liquefied carbonic acid gas throughout coal cargoes: but still the fires continued.

The *Palestine* burned, blew up, and tossed her crew into the sea. The old barque, faithful even then, gave good warning. There was plenty of time to have the ship's boats overboard, provisioned and watered, and she waited gently until she was passing placidly though quiet waters – the southeast coast of Sumatra near Palembang upon her port hand, Bangka

Island on the starboard – before the inferno in her hold finally blew up.

It is all in *Youth*. That in itself justifies the choice of ship and Conrad's whole long voyage. It was the fate of few voyages to be so splendidly chronicled, and the lot of few writers to take a most active part in such a quietly moving, long continued, drama of the sea. *Youth*, he called it. That crew was hardly youthful for its time. The average age was over 30. At 23 when he joined, Conrad himself was old for that sort of berth when second mates could qualify at 17.

But his story called *Youth* makes them all, and that inadequate old sailing collier, forever ageless.

Riversdale

By the end of August 1883, Conrad was back at last in London after his delayed but finally incendiary voyage on the *Palestine*. A fortnight later he had signed the articles of a 1,500-ton ship named *Riversdale* for a deepwater voyage of the standard duration of three years, in the first instance towards Algoa Bay, thence to anywhere accessible by sea between 70 degrees north latitude and 65 degrees south, the crew paying off anywhere on the Elbe–Brest range when she might show up there.

In her papers at that time, the *Riversdale*'s owner is listed as L. H. McIntyre, of 13 Union Court, Liverpool. Built in 1865, a composite (wooden planks on an iron or steel frame) full-rigged ship, she had made a number of Indian voyages during the late 1860s and early 1870s, and a Melbourne voyage in 1872 when she lost three able seamen, her carpenter and the ship's boy, probably swept overboard in the Roaring Forties. Captain R. Carter had earlier died (of epilepsy, says the entry in the official log) at the mouth of the Irrawaddy and was buried there by the mate, one Alex McKay. The articles show that half the crew could not sign their names, but this was more or less normal. Some might not have been sober at the time.

For the African–Indian voyage which began at London on 10 September 1883, Conrad – still Korzeniowski – signed as second mate at £5 5s the month. The master was an Aberdeen Scot by the name of Lawrence Brown McDonald, who was accompanied on the voyage by his wife and son, whose names were not recorded on the ship's articles as they should have been. The events of the voyage were to prove that Captain McDonald was as bad a master as Beard had been a good one.

After discharging her outward cargo in southern Africa, the *Riversdale* sailed to Madras, on a then open roadstead on the Bay of Bengal in southern India. Here, contrary to his original intention of completing a round voyage, Conrad signed off on 17 April 1884; and signed off, moreover, with a damning certificate of discharge. Under the column for 'ability for capacity engaged' Captain McDonald wrote 'v.g.', meaning very good, which was the standard comment. Under 'character for conduct', however, he wrote 'decline', meaning 'decline to report'.[5] This might have been disastrous for Conrad; his certificates of discharge were his only official record of his merchant naval career. Anything other than the formal v.g. under either category of character or capacity might impede heavily

---

5. The certificate is preserved at Yale University Library, New Haven, USA. Captain McDonald actually wrote 'decline' in the wrong section, but his intention is clear. Certificates of discharge, known as 'flimsies', were eventually replaced by a permanent discharge book.

or even blight his future career, by making it very difficult for him to get another ship.

Although the seaman, tradesman, or officer had no right of, or means to, appeal against anything which the ship's captain might say about him, captains differed greatly in their competence and abilities, and this was widely known in merchant naval circles. A bad discharge from Captain 'A' might be genuinely damning, whereas a bad discharge from Captain 'B', well known to be cranky, or dishonest, or (a much more popular category) an alcoholic, would be disregarded by other ship-masters and owners. A good many seamen were given bad discharges through no fault of their own, by a very few masters who would attempt, in this thoroughly despicable way, to cover up trouble which they themselves had caused.

As it happened, Conrad's sea-career was not blighted by his discharge in Madras, for Captain McDonald shortly afterwards established his own uselessness by stranding the *Riversdale*, and getting a very severe public rap over the knuckles in the subsequent official inquiry into his own conduct.

What were the facts at issue which led to McDonald's aspersion on his second mate? They could be summarised as follows: alcohol, incompetence, and dishonesty. Suffering a fit (probably delirium tremens) aboard his ship off Madras, Captain McDonald (or his mate, or his wife – the surviving documents are unclear) sent the second mate, Conrad, ashore to find a doctor named Thompson. With him, apparently, went another ship-master, a friend of McDonald. Rattling back to the waterfront in a gharry, Dr Thompson found out what he could of the case by questioning the second mate.

It seems that Conrad expressed the opinion that the master had had a fit of delirium tremens, for he was much given to drinking spirits and had already suffered many such fits during the voyage. This statement was passed on to McDonald, in due course, by his friend. Conrad was summarily fired and given a bad discharge to hinder him on his way. He left the *Riversdale* after writing a letter of apology for what he had said to Dr Thompson, and agreeing, as a final act of infamy on McDonald's part, to forfeit sixty rupees as expenses to which the ship would be put for having his place filled – an imposition which can be described only as bare-faced robbery. His place was never filled on those articles, but he received no refund. Always frugal at sea, he had paid off with 234 rupees, then about £23, from which he paid his fare to Bombay as a better port to find a ship.

It is perhaps an indication of the esteem in which McDonald was held by other captains that Conrad actually managed to obtain a new berth with no difficulty at all. Within a few days of leaving the *Riversdale*, he had signed on as second mate aboard the *Narcissus* at Bombay – a vastly better ship and master. Whether he produced his 'decline' flimsy is not known; in any case, it did not prevent him obtaining a new post.

Captain McDonald left Madras bound for the port of Vizagapatam (now called Vishakhapatam) without a second mate, but still, it would appear, with delirium tremens. The *Riversdale* never reached Vizagapatam, for she slipped very gently and very firmly ashore at False Divi Point, which was almost exactly halfway. She was far from her course

– not just a few miles off, but sixty, though she had then sailed little more than one hundred miles from Madras roads. An 'Extraordinary case of a stupid and unnecessary grounding', declared *Lloyd's List Weekly Summary & Shipping Gazette* in its issue for 17 October 1884. (By chance, this was the day that Conrad signed off the articles of the *Narcissus* at Dunkirk, on her arrival from Bombay.)

As was customary, two senior merchant-ship masters (by name Charles Reeves and John H. Roberts) were appointed to be assessors to assist the Special Court assembled at Madras on 24 June 1884. This sat until 8 July, to investigate the circumstances attending the stranding of the British ship *Riversdale* off False Point, Divi, on 29 April of that year. In the time during which the Inquiry probed thoroughly into all the circumstances of the wreck, those hard-bitten masters satisfied themselves about the state of discipline and efficiency aboard Captain McDonald's ship:

> We were struck by the remarkable nature of this shipwreck, unique in our experience. The *Riversdale* left port, experienced very fine weather, and in 24 hours glides quietly on shore without anyone on board being cognisant of that, and the first suspicion that anything was wrong was raised by her helmsman reporting that the ship was not steering. Draw a straight line between the place she left and the port she was bound to, and she is ashore 58 miles inside that line. Comment is superfluous.

Having said which, the court did, of course, express further comment. The assessors called 'particular attention to the position of the mate, Mr Arthur Johnson. The captain made no sort of confidant of him as regarded the position and navigation of the ship. The mate had neither access to the charts nor any means of knowing the ship's position. He seemed quite "sent to Coventry".' Even the chronometer readings for the occasional time-sight – the only method Captain McDonald practised for finding his longitude – were made by Mrs McDonald (perhaps because the chronometer belonged to her husband and was kept in the saloon, where apparently his wife and young son also lived). Therefore the mate 'could feel no sense of responsibility for anything in the ship.' McDonald, the assessors noted, had not even brought the chart he said he was using to the Inquiry, which he said he had left aboard, 'thinking it might be of use to anyone who got the ship off.'

The real reason would have been that it was absolutely clear of fixes, positions, bearings and other marks of the trade. By comparison, the ship's deck-log and official log, which had been produced for the Inquiry by law, showed such clumsy attempts at alteration that even Captain McDonald himself had to admit that alterations had been made, although at first denying this.

In suspending Captain McDonald's certificate of competence for twelve months, the court declared that:

> Either he did not now where he was going on that fine, clear night of normal current and favourable wind, in which case there was culpable recklessness: or he did not know where he was, which was both reckless and ignorant.

The mate's certificate was also suspended, but in his case only for three months: the court would have been aware that there was little that a first officer could do about such an incompetent master.

In regard to Captain McDonald's sobriety (or intoxication), both at the time of the accident and during the voyage as a whole, the court also found out the facts. Dr Thompson, whom Conrad had collected to attend the captain in Madras, stated that Conrad (described in the Inquiry as Mr Korzemowski: the first appearance of his name, or something like it, in print) had volunteered no information about Captain McDonald; his statements about excessive drinking and fits of delirium tremens were in response to Dr Thompson's own questions. Moreover, Mrs McDonald had given Conrad a note for the doctor, in which she expressed the same opinions as the second officer. Dr Thompson stated that he did not find a man suffering from delirium tremens. However, the ship's mate and sail-maker stated that the master drank to excess, and the seaman who was steering when the ship stranded said that the captain was not sober and was 'staggering about the deck'.

Captain McDonald, who was clearly not the sort of person to concede a lost cause, told the court that he had 'twice logged the second mate for sleeping on watch in Madras'. Even if this had been true, it was hardly a defence against his own recklessness, and in any case it did not make sense. What watch? The ship was anchored in a safe roadstead, so this must have been an 'anchor watch', kept in case the ship dragged. It was an informal sort of watch often entrusted to the youngest apprentice, who might be required to take cross-bearings and check the ship's position. It was not a task for the second mate. He would have been concerned with the cargo working and the ship's tally all day, although he was spared another of the second mate's normal duties, that of updating her charts, light lists, and so on, from the up-to-date *Notices to Mariners* to be collected from the British Consul. He saw no charts and Captain McDonald made no corrections.

McDonald's stranding of the *Riversdale* was considered so professionally disgraceful that it was widely reported in the shipping press, and the findings and report of proceedings of the Court of Inquiry at Madras were sent at once to the Board of Trade in London. Conrad, as a very interested party, would have had good reason to read all about it, for the Court's scathing comments made nonsense of his bad discharge from McDonald. A letter of Tadeusz Bobrowski congratulated Conrad on 'winning a case against his ex-captain'; this may refer simply to the findings of the Board of Inquiry v McDonald, reported by Conrad to Bobrowski.

The *Riversdale* was soon refloated from the shelf on which she grounded. Later she was stranded once again, this time on the coast of New Caledonia; and she finished her long life as an undistinguished coal-hulk in Sydney harbour, for Messrs J. and A. Brown.

Captain McDonald does not feature in maritime history again, although his licence was restored after twelve months: no doubt his disgrace was too damning.

There were McDonalds aplenty in the old sailing-ship days, with drink an ever-present temptation. There were no limits on the extent of the small company ship-master's duty-free stores, and his quarters were large: quite disproportionately so compared with all others aboard ship. With the best of Scotch available at a few shillings the large bottle, and rum even cheaper, the temptation was there. The captain could rig the accounts, if he wished, to finance a large store of liquor for himself – and then proceed to drink his way through it. Sadly, although Captain McDonald's incompetence and alcoholism were outstanding, he was far from the worst of his profession. Consider the voyage of the *Aberfoyle* from Norway to Australia, in which the captain drank himself to death at sea, allowing the *Aberfoyle* to be sailed for most of the rest of the voyage by a bos'n untrained in the science of navigation.[6]

For a balanced view, compare the outstanding record of Captain Woodget of the *Cutty Sark*, a true master mariner, as told by Alan Villiers in *The Way of a Ship*.[7]

---

6. Alan Villiers, *The War with Cape Horn*. Hodder & Stoughton, London, 1971, page 101.

7. Alan Villiers, *The Way of a Ship*. Charles Scribner's Sons, New York, 1970.

Narcissus

The ship *Narcissus*, in which Conrad shipped as second mate after the *Riversdale*, is certainly one he found for himself. Some of the others smack of prior arrangements, at least a 'tip-off', fruits of the laborious and loving probing of Uncle Tadeusz Bobrowski among his contacts, those distant countrymen exiled in Great Britain – but not the *Narcissus*. Conrad was sitting with some other merchant service officers on the veranda of the Sailors' Home in Bombay, overlooking the harbour, when he saw a sailing ship coming in, a lovely full-rigger with the grace of a perfect yacht. She was 235 feet long (216 feet at the waterline), with a short raised forecastle and poop and one deckhouse on the main deck; her beam amidships was 37 feet. She was the three-masted full-rigged ship *Narcissus*, a Scots-built vessel of 1,300 tons, and the date of her arrival at Bombay was 27 April 1884. Two days later Josef Konrad Korzeniowski was signed on as her second mate, for she had come from Penarth in South Wales without one, via South Africa, and apparently had no senior (or any other) apprentice, or educated boatswain to step into the berth. A William Evans had signed in Wales but failed to join.

As described officially, the *Narcissus* (ON 76149) of 1,336 gross and 1,270 net tons, built 1876 and registered at Greenock as owned by Robert R. Paterson of City Buildings there, had accommodation certified for fifty seamen. (Why so many? Perhaps she was expected to be manned by seamen listed overseas; often called Coolies if Chinese, or Lascars if Indian. A crew of twenty was enough, though four or six apprentices would have been handy.) The voyage, which except for the homeward passage was over when the Bombay wanderers signed on, was

> from Penarth to Cape Town and/or any ports or places within the limits of 75 Deg. North and 60 Deg. South Latitude, maximum period to be three years, trading in any rotation and to end in the UK or Continent, calling for orders where and when required: the ship to be regarded as fully manned with 20 all told, and one Indian rupee to be valued at two English shillings. (ship's articles)

The master's name was Archibald Duncan, born 1844 at Campbeltown, Scotland. He remained with the ship from start to finish of the full voyage. Her mate when she arrived at Bombay was Thomas Williams of Briton Ferry, who had signed for £7 7s a month. He was replaced at Bombay by Hamilton Hart of Hull, at £8, so that when the ship sailed from Bombay both watch-keepers, Hart and Korzeniowski, were new to her. No matter: she was bound on a southern summer run which should bring her off Good Hope in reasonable weather, though in the English Channel in bad. Sailing homewards from India at the right season came under the head of a 'flying-fish passage' in the hard-bitten deepwater seaman's world, for it was in great part of trade-winds run – right across the Indian Ocean with the trades as far as off Madagascar, and then round the Cape not far from the land with the Agulhas current to help. (Good Hope to them was always 'The Cape'; Cape Horn was 'The Horn'; all others save Hatteras and Flattery were not worth remembering). Then, with a bit of luck, there would be southerlies to blow the ship to the southeast trades of the Atlantic and more flying-fish weather, too good to be true! It would be necessary to work her through two lots of doldrums on the way, of course, crossing the Line twice, and maybe there would be three lots of horse latitudes if the ship was out of luck – but, on the whole, there was nothing really nasty to worry about until making for the English Channel in the end. Even there, anything westerly in the gales made them fair winds to run before, which was more or less simple sailing.

The six new able seamen signed at Bombay in May 1884, at £3 a month, included two Britons, a Norwegian from the American ship *Pharos*, a Channel Islander and a Scot named Archie McLean from the iron ship *County of Cardigan*. The sixth was probably named Joseph Barrow, for this is the name attested by X, his mark (a not unusual manner of signing on), from the four-masted ship *County of Dumfries* of Glasgow. His age is recorded as 35, and he was from Charlton County, Georgia, USA. He signed on during May, later than the others, and he is said to have been a black man. A Danish and a Portuguese AB had left the ship at Bombay. The Portuguese nationality in a deepwater limejuicer was almost as rare as a Pole, for the Portuguese had many ships of their own. The man may have been a Cape Verde Islander tired of Yankee whaling. His name is recorded as 'Antonio Carmo' as far as one may make out, born in 1857; his previous ship was the Canadian-built wooden barque *Knighton of Leith*. He signed off the *Narcissus* with a Dane named Andersen, and disappears.

Consular entries on the articles entered at Cape Town on the outward passage record desertions, an AB left there in prison, and another paid off 'B.M.C.' – by mutual consent, which could mean anything but at least indicated that the leaver had not been convicted of a crime.

This may seem a lot of crew changes when all hands had signed originally for a round voyage of three years, for the total number of men passing through the ship to maintain her crew at 20 hands before the mast adds up to 37. But this was better than usual for the period. The turnover of crew in British ships was often scandalous, mainly through desertions. Sailing-ship seamen, in British ships especially, were inveterate wanderers, often with a casual regard for the worth of the 'articles' they all must sign. There was reason for this, bound up with the economic effects of the decline of the sailing-ship era. These made manning a steadily worsening problem except in time of war, when freight boomed, the sailing ships earned good money, and owners and masters could afford to treat the men reasonably well. But between wars there was a steep decline affecting masters and officers as well as the foremast hands. Elderly sailing-ship masters, finding themselves compelled to serve in a declining industry, and being qualified only for that and too old to change, sometimes exploited their own crews with the idea of inducing their desertion, leaving their pay on the ship's books. The masters kept the accounts: many of the seamen were drifters of one sort of another, and could be induced to leave the ship, to the master's profit.[8]

On the face of it, the *Narcissus* was a good ship, 'born in the thundering peal of hammers beating upon iron, in black eddies of smoke under a grey sky, on the banks of the Clyde', as Conrad wrote in his novel *The Nigger of the Narcissus*, completed in 1897, and using the name of a real ship in a work of fiction:

> The clamorous and sombre stream gives birth to things of beauty that float away into the sunshine of the world to be loved by men. The *Narcissus* was one of that perfect brood. (*Nigger of the Narcissus*, chapter 3)

To judge by the length of her passage on the voyage, she was not fast – or perhaps not well sailed, maybe not handled by a man with that priceless gift of keeping his ship in good sailing winds. The records show that she had taken 76 days to reach her African port and another 90 thence to Bombay. These were straightforward ocean passages, far simpler than many, and might have been faster. 'She was at times rather crank,' said Conrad, 'requiring careful loading and handling.' Well, all square-rigged ships demanded that. There is no doubt that the *Narcissus* was an attractive ship with a graceful and nobly proportioned hull.

According to the articles of agreement, the *Narcissus* took 130/135 days to return from Bombay to England. During this final leg died Joseph Barrow, the American sailor from Georgia who had signed on in Bombay. The cause of death is unknown as the ship's official log, which was Barrow's only official death certificate, has long been destroyed. For the same reason it is not known if any particular episode took place during this passage which might have been recorded in the official log.

Those are the facts concerning Conrad's passage in the *Narcissus*, in so far as they can be verified. Conrad went on to use this ship's name and voyage, and the death during it of a black member of the crew, in his story *The Nigger of the Narcissus*. Some early biographers, perhaps more knowledgeable about literature than the sea, assumed this work to be based entirely on the factual voyage of the *Narcissus*. Jean-Aubry, for example, described *The Nigger of the Narcissus* as 'nothing but the realistic and lyrical account of the ship's actual voyage'.

This is not so. *The Nigger of the Narcissus* is not a true account of experiences the author underwent at sea. He wrote fiction, said Conrad years later in conversation with his French biographer: he was entitled to select, to edit, to enlarge upon, or tone down, the realities of his voyages. He certainly did so in the case of the voyage of the *Narcissus*. His actual words, according to Jean-Aubry, were as follows:

---

8. See Alan Villiers, *The War with Cape Horn* (Hodder and Stoughton, London, 1971) for evidence of gross mistreatment of seamen, including 'forced' desertions. See also James Fell, *British Merchant Seamen in San Francisco, 1892–1898* (E. Arnold, London, 1899).

As you know, I do not write history, but fiction, and I am therefore entitled to choose as I please in what is most suitable in regard to characters and particulars to help me in the general impression I wish to produce.[9]

This is how Conrad describes the passage of the *Narcissus* towards the Cape of Good Hope from India:

> The passage had begun; and the ship, a fragment detached from the earth, went on lonely and swift like a small planet ... A great circular solitude moved with her, ever changing and ever the same, always monotonous and always imposing ... The august loneliness of her path lent dignity to the sordid inspiration of her pilgrimage. She drove foaming to the southward as if guided by the courage of high endeavour. (*Nigger of the Narcissus*, chapter 2)

All this presumably in the perfect sailing conditions of summer in the Indian Ocean north of the Line, when the gloriously fair wind of the northeast monsoon sped the great European homeward-bound square-riggers towards the Cape, to swing past there and sail northwards and northwest into the southeast trades. And so the ship sped on, and the crew prepared for stormy weather, which came soon enough:

> Then again, with a fair wind and under a clear sky, the ship went on piling up the South Latitude. They passed outside Madagascar and Mauritius without a glimpse of the land. Extra lashings were put on the spare spars. Hatches were looked to. The steward in his leisure moments and with a worried air tried to fit washboards to the cabin doors. Stout canvas was bent with care. Anxious eyes looked to the Westward, towards the cape of storms. The ship began to dip into a southwest swell, and the softly luminous sky of low latitudes took on a harder sheen from day to day above our heads: it arched high above the ship vibrating and pale, like an immense dome of steel, resonant with the deep voice of freshening gales. The sunshine gleamed cold on the white curls of black waves. Before the strong breath of westerly squalls the ship, with reduced sail, lay slowly over, obstinate and yielding. She drove to and fro in the unceasing endeavour to fight her way through the invisible violence of the winds: she pitched headlong into dark smooth hollows; she struggled upwards over the snowy ridges of great running seas; she rolled, restless, from side to side, like a thing in pain. Enduring and valiant, she answered to the call of men; and her slim spars, waving for ever in abrupt semicircles, seemed to beckon in vain for help towards the stormy sky. (*Nigger of the Narcissus*, chapter 3)

The weather steadily worsened:

> The ship tossed about, shaken furiously, like a toy in the hand of a lunatic ... Out of the abysmal darkness of the black cloud overhead white hail streamed on her, rattled on the rigging, leaped in handfuls off the yards, rebounded off the deck – round and gleaming in the turmoil like a shower of pearls. It passed away. For a moment a livid sun shot horizontally the last rays of sinister light between the hills of steep, rolling waves. Then a wild night rushed in – stamped out in a great howl that distant remnant of a stormy day. There was no sleep on board that night. Most seamen

---

9. Gérard Jean-Aubry (ed.), *Joseph Conrad: Life and Letters.* Doubleday, New York, 1927. The editor notes that this information was supplied by Joseph Conrad in June 1924.

remember in their life one or two such nights of a culminating gale. Nothing seems left of the whole universe but darkness, clamour, fury – and the ship. (*Nigger of the Narcissus*, chapter 3)

Next morning, off the Cape of Good Hope, the gale still continued, and a combination of wind and sea half-capsized the *Narcissus*, leaving her on her side. Conrad describes it as follows:

A big, foaming sea came out of the mist: it made for the ship, roaring wildly, and in its rush it looked as mischievous and discomposing as a madman with an axe ... It towered close to and high, like a wall of green glass topped with snow. The ship rose to it as though she had soared on wings, and for a moment rested poised upon the foaming crest as if she had been a great sea-bird. Before we would draw breath a heavy gust struck her, another follower took her unfairly under the weather bow, she gave a toppling lurch, and filled her decks. (*Nigger of the Narcissus*, chapter 3)

So the ship is flung on her side, goes over on her beam-ends, and hangs there, half her long hull immersed in the sea, for an unconscionably lengthy period of time. The master refuses to allow the masts to be cut away, so that the ship's hull might right itself. The crew expect the ship to turn turtle at any moment, but she does not. The black man, James Wait, has been sick and is confined to a different part of the ship from the rest of the crew in the foc's'l, in a cabin on deck. He is rescued from his cabin, which has become a trap with the ship on its side. The storm continues. And eventually the ship recovers from her disaster. The crew are able to 'wear ship' to some extent even whilst she is on her beam-ends; she pulls herself through and then out of the water, and continues her voyage, undamaged, unchanged. Nothing has carried away. Nothing is lost but some sails, and some of the contents of the forecastle, and some of the ship's stores.

During the remainder of the voyage human events take first place. There is a near-mutiny of the crew over the master's alleged ill-treatment of James Wait, the dying seaman, which Captain Allistoun quells with an extraordinary display of unbending authority. The black man eventually dies within sight of land, as Singleton, oldest and wisest AB on board, had predicted he would. The *Narcissus* reaches port; the crew pays off; the story ends.

It is a fine and moving story. It is a measure of Conrad's genius that he writes so realistic and evocative an account of the *Narcissus*'s capsize that we are able to believe in it absolutely. For the blowing-over of the *Narcissus* should not have occurred; and, had it happened, it would have been impossible for the ship to resurrect itself and sail on with masts intact. It is in this sense that Jean-Aubry's comment that *The Nigger of the Narcissus* is nothing more than a 'realistic and lyrical account of the ship's actual voyage' is wrong. Such accidents had happened – *did* happen often enough, right to the end of the great sailing-ship era. There was, for one example, the German school-ship *Pamir* which went down on her side for ever in a hurricane off the Azores in 1957, taking nearly all her crew of ninety with her.

But such blowings-over cannot happen without a cause. The *Pamir* was badly laden with a cargo – loose barley – which could shift and run like sand. It did not fill her; it was not safely stowed; when it slipped the big barque slipped, too, and she could not get up again. She was an auxiliary (unlike any square-rigged ship that Conrad sailed in) with engine-room skylights and dangerous but then essential deck-openings which (when she began to fall over) could let the sea enter. Ships like the *Narcissus*, which were deep-loaded, full of good cargo well stowed, had no such openings. Hatches battened down, caulked, triple-tarpaulined and breakwatered let no sea in. Everything and everybody was above decks, the afterguard aft, the seamen for'ard, in structures stoutly built at her ends – in the *Narcissus* her forecastle-head (the traditional seamen's quarters in old-fashioned ships; later the men lived in stout steel houses on deck) and the poop, commodious and invulnerable in a ship properly prepared for sea.

Provided the cargo (or ballast, if she were sailing in ballast) could not and did not shift, then the undamaged ship ought never to go on her beam-ends. The *Narcissus* was undamaged. The cargo and its stowage are not mentioned, but no-one goes into the hold. (There was a safe inspection-spot aft, accessible from the after-quarters, usually by the steward's store-room.) So the ship would not have been blown over and stayed on her side in the sea.

Had, somehow, the *Narcissus* gone on her beam-ends, she would never have recovered. She might have gone over a little, and come out of it; but to fall down and stay down (with no cargo shift or anything of that kind), then get up again, and shake herself free of the sea, like some great Newfoundland dog – no. This is the supreme work of the inspired imagination, in which we are able to suspend our disbelief. During the storm off the Cape of Good Hope we ceased to sail with Conrad the seaman, and began to sail with Conrad the novelist. The second mate of the real *Narcissus* has become the marvellously inspired and imaginative writer who was to use his experience as a basis for fiction. As Conrad himself was to write many years later, in *A Personal Record* (page 25):

> Only in men's imagination does every truth find an effective and undeniable existence. Imagination, not invention, is the supreme master of art as of life. An imaginative and exact rendering of authentic memories may serve worthily that spirit of piety towards all things human which sanctions the conceptions of a writer of tales, and the emotions of a man reviewing his own experience.

Narcissus maintained a shadowy presence in Conrad's subsequent seafaring. Thirty years after leaving her at Dunkirk he saw her for the last time – if indeed he noticed her at all, for he had much else to preoccupy him at the time. Escaping from Austrian-occupied Poland during the first weeks of war in 1914, he took his family home to England on board a Dutch mail-boat homeward-bound from the east, at Genoa. Moored in the harbour at Genoa lay the hulk of the once proud Glaswegian ship *Narcissus*, now under Italian ownership.[10] *Narcissus* went back to sea in 1916, re-rigged as a barque, wearing the flag of Brazil and

10. Jerry Allen, *The Sea Years of Joseph Conrad*. Doubleday, New York, 1965, pages 169, 321.

the name *Isis*: during war-time, all shipping is at a premium and any vessel may be called back into service. She was hulked for the last time in 1925, and ended her days as a worn-out hulk in Rio de Janeiro harbour in the 1930s. Like other good ships she kept her grace of hull and her proud and perfect proportions even in those circumstances. Alan Villiers saw her there when exercising the lifeboats of the ship *Joseph Conrad* in Rio harbour early in 1935. He wrote that:

> The name then on the shapely counter, *Isis*, meant nothing to me, but I asked the ship-chandler with whom I dealt in Rio (who chanced to be a fellow-townsman from Melbourne) if he knew anything of the ship. He told me she had been the *Narcissus*, and that he had had some shares in her as the Brazilian *Isis*, years earlier. She had sunk through collision, not by wearing out.

Many years later, Captain Villiers looked again, but the beautiful harbour of Rio was much changed, with the emphasis now on cars to cross the bay at speed, not for ships to lie safely at anchor. He could not find the *Isis* again, nor anyone who had heard of her.

Tilkhurst

Despite the outrageous treatment he had received from the master of the ship *Riversdale* and the long passage homewards in the *Narcissus*, Conrad took a liking to the East, apparently, for his following two ships were in that trade. The advantages were obvious – more interesting ports in fascinating countries, especially for a man such as he was; easier (on the whole) voyages with more use of the pleasant trade-wind zones of the sailing ships' world, not too much cold and wet 'running the easting down', and no need to battle with those notorious headlands of the square-riggers' passage-making – Hatteras, Flattery, or Killer Number One, the Horn. Conrad never took on the Horn to wind'ard. His experience there consisted of a couple of downhill summer runs from Australia, which the old copper-ore men and the nitrate traders scarcely counted as Cape Horn roundings at all. He was never (after those few preliminary French experiences) in a ship sailing to a port anywhere in all North or South America, east coast or west coast, although such ports kept probably half the larger sailing ships in the world going through at least three-fourths of the nineteenth century, as well as large numbers also in the first decade of the twentieth. Well, a seaman went where his ships went, and what happened was the luck of the game. The great majority of the world's large square-rigged ships were essentially tramps.

It was more than six months after returning in the *Narcissus* before Conrad shipped out again at all. According to data listed by himself on his application to be examined for a certificate of competency as master, filed at Tower Hill in London in November 1886, he left the *Narcissus* on 17 October 1884, and did not sign the articles of the *Tilkhurst* until 5 June 1885, nearly eight months later. This was a very long break for a professional merchant-service officer at a time when ships were plentiful and doing well. What was he doing? Thinking things out? Conrad very often gives one the impression of being a gifted and most unusual young man following the sailing-ship sea for his own very personal reasons, not as a maritime career at all. He seemed to pause after each ship, absorbing the experience for its own worth, not at all to do with his own advancement as a world-wandering seafarer.

We also know from his correspondence with his uncle that while he enjoyed the life at sea, in many ways conditions in the British merchant service were a considerable shock to Conrad. This, together with the miserable pay which a merchant-service officer received, meant that between ships Conrad would devote some time at least to considering other careers, or at least to ways of improving his income. He considered various business ventures in London; he also looked into the possibility of going whaling as a commercial venture, borrowing capital, buying a ship, and catching whales, and keeping the profits, rather than doing it all for a pittance. However, the whaling venture came to nothing, which was perhaps just as well. Greenland whaling offered the world's most savage testing-ground for the world's toughest seamen. Profits were high, but so were deaths.

Conrad did make one solid achievement during this period ashore in connection with his merchant-service career – he sat and passed his examination for mate or chief officer. Most other nations which had a large merchant marine had examinations for only one grade of deep-sea mate, and the next step was to master. Britain was unusual in requiring candidates to pass as second mates first, then as chief mates later, but having passed for the lower grade the test for the higher was by no means formidable. In the interval the candidate had to serve at least a year as a watch-keeping second mate in an ocean-going ship: Conrad had done far more, and the only voyage he had had to waste was that with the dour old Scot in the *Loch Etive*. This makes no appearance on his qualifying papers, for he had ample time in without that.

It is unlikely that he required much time to prepare for that middle step: the later (and final) advancement to master was a much more significant one, and the mate's examination was generally considered the easiest of the three.

Conrad gained his first mate's certificate on 3 December 1884, though not without some difficulty. He later wrote ironically of his sardonic examiner, in *A Personal Record* (page 115):

> He kept inscrutably silent for a moment, and then, placing me in a ship of a certain size at sea ... ordered me to execute a certain manoeuvre. Before I was half way through it he did some material damage to the ship. Directly I had grappled with the difficulty he caused another to present itself, and when that too was met he stuck another ship before me, creating a very dangerous situation. I felt slightly outraged by this ingenuity in piling up trouble upon a man.
>
> 'I wouldn't have got into that mess,' I suggested mildly. 'I could have seen that ship before.' He never slurred the least bit.
>
> 'No, you wouldn't. The weather's thick.'
>
> 'Oh! I didn't know,' I apologised blankly.

The ordeal continued. Long before the end, Conrad wrote, he would have welcomed an opportunity to exchange into the *Flying Dutchman*. But he passed.

The ship *Tilkhurst* was a tramp, an iron three-master of 1,528 tons, belonging to the firm of W. R. Price of London. She was built by the well-known firm of McMillan & Son at Dumbarton on the Clyde in 1877, and was thus only a few years old when Conrad joined her. She was one of those splendidly tough Scots square-riggers, graceful and gracious, with a fine hull to make good passages, but big enough to stow a paying cargo as well. Moreover, as an early iron ship, she was almost indestructible; had she been looked after, the *Tilkhurst* could still have been in existence a century later. The early iron hulls were built more stoutly and strongly than was really necessary; the lighter steel ships which came later could stow more, and so earn more, and thus iron was quickly outmoded.

The master of the *Tilkhurst* was as good as his ship. He was a Plymouth (England) seaman named Edwin J. Blake who had served his time in small, incredibly tough Welsh barques and ships known as the 'Swansea copper-ore men'. These were rough little battlers whose trade year-in year-out was between south Wales and the Chilean ore ports, coal out and ore home, taking on the Horn summer or winter both ways – to wind'ard outwards, with the wild westerlies fair (on the whole) homewards. These were the ships where the rough, tough ABs were said to cut spare rope-yarns from their heads and beards as necessary, and find all the seizing-wire they needed growing on their chests! (And very little exaggeration in that – doubtless they drove in caulking irons with their bare hands, too.) They were utterly courageous and thoroughly competent seamen, bred hard and clear-minded.

With *that* sort of beginning, Captain Blake should have found the *Tilkhurst* voyage a rest cure, and so he would have done had he not been suffering from problems with his health, which broke down on the ship's homeward passage. Nevertheless, he was both an excellent seaman and a man whom Conrad could like and admire. He wrote a short tribute to Captain Blake many years later, in his book of memoirs and impressions, *The Mirror of the Sea* (page 9):

> Well over fifty years of age when I knew him, short, stout, dignified, perhaps a little pompous, he was a man of a singularly well-informed mind, the least sailor-like in outward aspect, but certainly one of the best seaman whom it has been my good luck to serve under.

The *Tilkhurst* made a reasonable and uneventful passage from Penarth in south Wales outwards to Singapore with a full cargo of coal (5 June to 22 September, 110 days); and thence to Calcutta to load jute for Dundee. Sailing the homeward leg of the voyage seems to have taken at least a month longer; she was not back discharging in Dundee until June 1886 – a twelve-month for one round voyage. But with two freights and reasonable working costs both in Singapore and Calcutta, the *Tilkhurst* should have earned a reasonable if not extravagant dividend for that year.

On Conrad's homeward passage, an able seaman was drowned. According to the entry in the log, this man – one William Cummings – had been injured on the head in a drunken brawl at Singapore and fell overboard at sea one night, in a delirium. The injury's effects had apparently worsened, poor fellow. It was a very easy matter for a seaman to be lost overboard by night from a big square-rigger, even in good weather. The unfortunate Cummings was handicapped at the time, and laid up. The only way he could relieve himself was to shuffle out on deck and along to the heads for'ard, or climb on the lee pin-rail in the waist along the bulwarks, and pump ship overboard into the sea. Here he might have no hold, little balance: a lurch and he was gone, with the ship sailing past him before he surfaced again. Nothing was lit save a binnacle lamp, both for economy and the preservation of the men's night vision; and watches were checked by night only at eight bells' muster, which the sick did not attend.

The *Tilkhurst* arrived at Dundee in mid June 1886, and Conrad paid off with £29.15.8½d accumulated pay, having been a year and a few days on her articles. He travelled down to London with Captain Blake and his wife. The captain offered him a berth in the future, but as it turned out this was his last voyage; and so this friendly and useful offer came to nothing.

As for the *Tilkhurst*, she lasted well into the twentieth century. She was still carrying full 100 A1 class at Lloyd's in 1913, when she was sailing as the *Blanche*, for Giuseppe Mortola of Genoa. By this time the *Blanche* had been reduced to barque rig by the simple process of sending down the yards on the mizzen, and the fore and main royal yards. She sailed just as well. She was never a record-breaker, nor meant to be; just a well-balanced and reliable workhorse of the sea, strong, safe, and of good spirit. One likes to think that among others both Captain Blake and Second Officer Korzeniowski made their contribution to this.

Highland Forest

Conrad established himself in his usual lodgings in Stoke Newington, London, and began to prepare for the final examination of his merchant-navy career – his master's ticket. Although he would not necessarily gain a command immediately he had this, it was customary for the brighter merchant-navy officer to obtain, or try to obtain, his master's ticket as soon as he had the necessary sea-time. In those days when there were no pensions to receive, or welfare state to rely on, a master might remain at sea into his eighties, simply because he had no other means of support. Under those circumstances it was as well for the mate to be prepared for command, for it might be sprung on him at any moment.

Conrad's uncle Tadeusz Bobrowski, always both practical and far-sighted, had understood the structure of the British merchant navy clearly enough, and encouraged Conrad all along to become fully qualified in his chosen profession. He had also been urging Conrad for years to become naturalised as British, so that imperial Russia would never be able to claim him. Now, at last, Conrad became a British subject, in August 1886, eight years after his arrival in Lowestoft. Conrad Korzeniowski of the British merchant navy was a very different man from the unthinking youth who had run up large debts in Marseille, whilst toying with the idea of becoming a professional seaman. His uncle wrote that he was really delighted by the news, as well he might have been; he too had waited a long time for it. Now at last the nephew about whom he had worried so much had proved himself. He was on course, under full sail. Well done!

In February 1887 Conrad signed as mate in another tramp square-rigger – this time the barque *Highland Forest* of Glasgow, of a little over 1,000 tons. A barque was a three-masted vessel differing from the full-rigged ship in that her mizzen mast carried only fore-and-aft sails, making her much simpler to handle. Conrad joined the ship in the port of Amsterdam, then ice-bound, and was put to a rather severe test as the thaw began. Her cargo came down to the basin where she lay – very mixed general for Samarang in Java – and in the absence of Captain McWhirr on home leave, the mate had to load it, which meant seeing to the cargo's stowage and the ship's trim, both vital matters for her sailing and her safety.

It was the first general cargo for which he had been responsible. The more usual full load of coal was no problem, but general cargo in boxes, crates, bales, and so forth, all of different weights and capacities, was quite a complicated stowage problem. The *Duke of Sutherland* and the *Loch Etive* were general cargo carriers, but he joined both in London shortly before they sailed with their hatches battened down and ready to go: and in Sydney loading had been none of his responsibility. The *Highland Forest*'s full hold contained crated machinery and all sorts of things of greatly varying weights and sizes. A sailing ship was one large hold, deep, dark and cavernous: but one had to be very careful indeed how one filled it. Ships had their idiosyncrasies, their individual stability problems, and their own requirements for trim. Some were like old draught horses and others lean racing beasts, high-strung, inclined to be ultra-sensitive. How could one know before a voyage? There was rarely any data aboard, no trim-tables, stability curves, old cargo-plans – nothing like that, not even hearsay from some intelligent survivor of the ship's last crew. Nor was the general subject studied in any depth for the three grades of deck officers' certificates of competence in those days, which by comparison with other nations' examinations were rather primitive, it has to be said.

There was the cargo alongside the *Highland Forest* in fat barges from inland, the ice having opened enough for loading, with large, florid men clamouring for it to be put aboard, and more and more barges and large canal boats coming with more. And no sign of the experienced and knowledgeable Captain McWhirr. The stuff had to be loaded and stowed. Detaining barges cost money. So Conrad got on with it, probably glad that at least it was all for the one port, Samarang. He did his best and he was no sort of fool.

However, in his ignorance of the *Highland Forest*'s particular characteristics, he loaded her wrongly, as Captain McWhirr indicated to him when he eventually joined, just as the loading had been completed. Conrad described this in *The Mirror of the Sea* (page 52):

> Without further preliminaries than a friendly nod he addressed me: 'You have got her pretty well in her fore and aft trim. Now, what about your weights?'
>
> I told him I had managed to keep the weight sufficiently well up, as I thought, one third of the whole being in the upper part 'above the beams', as the technical expression has it. He whistled 'Phew!' scrutinizing me from head to foot. A sort of smiling vexation was visible on his ruddy face.
>
> 'Well, we shall have a lively time of it this passage, I bet,' he said … He was right in his prophecy … Neither before nor since have I felt a ship roll so abruptly, so violently, so heavily. Once she began you felt she would never stop.

That passage to the East consisted in the usual tremendous non-stop sail of 8,000 miles or more. Down through both Atlantics with the doldrums to defeat between them (and any swell in otherwise calm waters there) would make a badly loaded square-rigger lurch like a drunkard. The southeast trade wind on her port beam for two weeks or more would force her over towards the coast of Brazil (which more than a few southbound square-riggers actually sailed into and were wrecked on). Then she could swing southeastwards towards the wild westerlies, and run before those – 4,000 miles in the Roaring Forties – before she turned north towards the Straits of Sunda. Conrad wrote:

> Down south, running before the gales of high latitudes, she made our life a burden to us ... She rolled and rolled with an awful dislodging jerk and that dizzily fast sweep of her masts on every swing. It was a wonder that the men sent aloft were not flung off the yards, the yards not flung off the masts, the masts not flung overboard. The captain in his armchair, holding on grimly at the head of the table, with the soup-tureen rolling on one side of the cabin and the steward sprawling on the other, would observe, looking at me: 'That's your one third above the beams. The only thing that surprises me is that the sticks have stuck to her all this time.' (*Mirror of the Sea*, page 54)

Ultimately some of the minor spars did go; and, by a form of poetic justice, poor Conrad was the one to suffer for it. A 'piece of one of the minor spars' (perhaps a yardarm plug, or a piece of a studding-sail boom) fell from aloft and smote him in the back. Conrad was lucky not to be killed; but he was seriously injured. He had to go straight to hospital when the *Forest* reached Samarang.

This was in early July 1887. Samarang was very much the outpost then; somehow the injured Conrad made his way to a larger hospital in Singapore, which was much more a part of the world. A serious accident of some sort, sooner or later, was more or less the accepted thing in the sailing-ship seaman's life, particularly in the ocean-going square-rigger, in those days. Like other seamen, he was philosophical about it. Now that he might have real need of it, the Bobrowski allowance had stopped. That good man had other obligations. No matter: being of no use to her for some time to come, Conrad was paid off the barque with £10 or so, and could be officially regarded as a 'Distressed British Seaman', which gave consuls an interest in him and a duty not to see him quite stranded.

For the time being at least, he was not badly off. Singapore was an excellent place for the qualified man to find a ship to his liking, for then as now the fascinating port was centre of a great network of little wandering vessels scouring the pleasant seas of the East, picking up and putting down cargoes. The Samarang medico had prescribed three months of quiet for him, on his back, which was a luxury for anyone come from a deep-sea ship, and bliss to someone who had been in the incessantly rolling *Highland Forest*.

It seems that the spar-struck mate of the *Highland Forest*, if not soon on his feet again, was at any rate quickly established in an excellent room overlooking part of the harbour, towards Singapore Roads – probably as fascinating a stretch of ship-filled waterway as the world provides, then and now.

Here he was soon making friends. He was a most unusual merchant-service officer, with his quietly distinguished air of the aristocracy, his reserved but friendly manner, his swift and wide-ranging mind – and his almost self-denying inclination to choose a ship for its personal appeal, rather than for its place on his CV. As for that, it soon turned out that his interesting and eventful career was not at an end – far from it. It was merely changed. Inside two months, without apparently ever finding out what ailed him from that clout with the piece of a spar, Conrad was not only on his feet again but finding himself a ship, and an extremely interesting little ship, too.

She was the *Vidar*, a coasting steamer of some 400 tons, commanded by a competent, interesting and friendly Scot, by name David Craig. Conrad was rather lucky to get such a berth. He was in his late 20s, a qualified master, but in fact, compared with many if not most of his contemporaries, he had not been at sea for very long. He had scarcely been in powered vessels as a working seaman at all, and never as an officer. The brief early jaunt in the small steamer *Mavis* was mainly if not entirely for passage. Moreover, the *Vidar* was a specialist trader in waters considered dangerous to those not thoroughly familiar with them. But Conrad got along well with Captain David Craig from their first meeting, which was in the Mercantile Marine office at Singapore in August 1887. After all, Craig had local knowledge enough for the two of them, and the *Vidar* belonged to a benevolent old Arab who left maritime technicalities to his captain. She was not on an arduous schedule, though regular, and was well manned and maintained. Craig, it seems, had a bit of a financial interest in the *Vidar* as well as commanding her. He would have been pleased to choose as his new mate, not only someone who might be expected to learn quickly, but a professional seaman who had not developed an insatiable taste for alcohol – an all-too-common failing of ships' officers in tropical waters.

If those East Indies waters were rough spots for the novice to learn his pilotage and ship-handling in, they were warm, clean and predictable with their monsoonal rhythm, and friendly. So were the *Vidar* and her Scots master. Captain Craig was an observant man with an encyclopaedic knowledge not only of the maritime side of his trade but also of the fascinating variety of colourful persons in it. Conrad was very fortunate to obtain the berth, indeed – both from the point of view of his merchant naval career, and for his subsequent career as a writer.

It is significant that the quietly observant Captain Craig speaks of his mate as a writing man – writing, writing, writing when relieved from his watch even long after midnight: not writing letters. Writing? Of course he was. The *Vidar* was a picturesque old ship, and picturesque, colourful and fantastic characters crowded aboard into her at almost every landing-stage in her winding journeys. One person in particular whom Conrad met through the *Vidar* was a Dutch (or Eurasian) trader named William Olmeijer, who became the Almayer of Conrad's first book, *Almayer's Folly*. Conrad later wrote (in *A Personal Record*, chapter 4):

> If I had not got to know Almayer pretty well [he meant Olmeijer] it is almost certain that there would never have been a line of mine in print.

Conrad was able to use his period in the *Vidar* in several of his other books as well, including *An Outcast of the Islands*, *Lord Jim*, *Victory* and *The Rescue*, both for background and for ideas for characters and plots.

Conrad served in the *Vidar* for less than five months. Through the eyes and in the mind of anyone else, they might have seemed rather uneventful months. Nothing much really happened, save in him. Suddenly he left the ship – chucked his berth, he said, feeling like a man walking out on a good wife for no satisfactory reason. Restlessness, perhaps? He had known plenty of that. Captain Craig, astonished at first, perhaps dismayed, seemed to understand. It must have been clear to him very quickly that his Polish mate was no ordinary career seafaring man – no ordinary man at all.

So on a day very early in 1888, Mr Mate Korzeniowski signed off the articles of the steamship *Vidar* at Singapore, collected his pay and his sea-bag, walked down her gangplank, and took a cab to the Sailors' Home. Here, in a bright, clear officer's room giving a fine prospect of the fascinating harbour, he settled in. Why? Waiting for what? He cannot have known.

Was it the result of some psychic feeling, some curious 'hunch' perhaps? Such had happened before in his career. Whatever the cause, he knew that he had given up a good berth in a fine little steamship with an excellent master. But he had never really approached his seafaring life as a professional career – not in any ordinary way – and he was making no change in that attitude now. So it might have been a psychic feeling of swiftly approaching change, a strange awareness.

There he was, financially sound enough to afford a rest, a professional ship's officer entitled to some quiet content, looking back over his rather unusual career, and looking forward with a clean record and some wide experience, ready, and he hoped qualified, for whatever might next turn up. In that port something certainly would. He could be sure of that.

He was ashore perhaps ten days when suddenly there was a message for him. The King's Harbour Master of Singapore would like to see him urgently, and there was some hint of a command. Of what? Conrad called a gharry and made at once for the Harbour Master's office, his eyes searching the waterfront, the Roads, the harbour along the way for some possible hint as to which ship this might be. He was sure of one thing. It had to be a sailing-ship, a square-rigger. But the drive seemed to offer no clue of a suitable ship at all.

Otago

There was no suitable ship in view in Singapore harbour, for she had docked in Bangkok. Her name was *Otago*, she was an iron-hulled barque of about 400 tons, she had been built in 1869, and she was in immediate need of a new master because Captain Snadden, who was also her managing owner, had died at sea – if not under suspicious circumstances, then at least under conditions that gave grounds for some confusion.

The *Otago* had cleared from Newcastle, New South Wales on 8 August 1887, bound for Haiphong with coal under Captain Snadden. She arrived at Haiphong on 29 October 1887, discharged her coal, took on ballast, and sailed for Hong Kong on 22 November 1887. Snadden died on 8 December 1887, and was buried at sea off Vietnam – this event would have been recorded in the official log. The ship was now equidistant between Bangkok and Singapore and her mate as acting master had to decide what to do. In the absence of the ship's master, who had also had charge of its business affairs, where should he take the ship?

On Snadden's death the ship became the property of Henry Simpson and Sons of Adelaide, South Australia, who had already been part-owners with Captain Snadden. Nowadays, the mate – he was an Australian of German origin called Bohn, usually anglicised to Born – would have been able to contact the owners by instant means and refer the decision to them. In 1887, no such action was possible. Cables existed on land, but there was no means of communicating from ship to shore save by flag or semaphore, and that required line of sight. What to do had to be decided unaided, by the man on the spot.

Mr Born decided, and as acting master brought the ship to Bangkok. Singapore would have been a more sensible alternative for a ship in need of a new master, for Singapore was a much busier port than Bangkok. Moreover, as a British possession Singapore had a port authority able to regulate British shipping in these matters. However, the mate would appear to have had his motives. If he were hoping to be offered command himself, there was unlikely to be a qualified and temporarily unemployed master simply sitting waiting in Bangkok for what might arise. Mr Born hoped, no doubt, that in such pressing circumstances the ship's owners might confirm his acting command – especially as he had immediately signed a charter to take logs to Australia.

If such were the mate's hopes he was doomed to be disappointed. There were indeed no local candidates in Bangkok, and as the *Otago* had to complete her new charter the need for a replacement was urgent. But it seemed that her mate was recommended only by himself, and in any case lacked the necessary master's certificate. The ship's owners made appropriate use of the simple invention of the telegraph to communicate with the appropriate authority in Singapore, where the professional merchant-navy officer Konrad Korzeniowski happened to be without a ship. Conrad's master's certificate – deepwater, square-rigged, any tonnage – was in order. His references from his employers were good. Wages were to be £14 a month. Would he accept the berth? Indeed he would.

Within a day or two Conrad was on his way by coastal steamer towards the river port of Bangkok in Siam, where the *Otago* was lying, right in the heart of that fascinating old river-port. This was a real chance. Command! He was offered command of a real, ocean-going, square-rigged ship: more than that, he was on his way to take over, to see his barque properly laden and sail her from Siam to Australia and afterwards to wherever she might be bound.

This was excellent: but there could be problems. There must be some. The coastal steamer (paid for under his new terms of engagement) took four days to reach Bangkok from Singapore; Conrad had plenty of time for reflection. He may have reflected that, compared with many of his contemporaries, he had really had very little experience; and that the jump from mate to actual command was a very considerable one. His experience as an officer at sea was short. He had been third mate for one voyage on the *Loch Etive* but not in charge of a watch, except for one brief period of fine weather. He had been second mate in four deepwater men but had completed a round voyage on one ship only, the *Tilkhurst*. He had been mate once only and that for half a voyage. True, he had satisfactory references from all his masters (except for the drunken and incompetent master of the *Riversdale*, who had disgraced himself and did not count). But it was still a very short preparation for independent command.

The gap was made still wider between master and mate because most masters never allowed their mates to handle the ships they sailed, except in the deadest of doldrums. The usual thing was that the master did all the handling that mattered. The two mates were his eyes, his aides, his alternating watch-keepers: in a sense and in many ships, they were foremen rather than officers. The master put the ship about by tacking or wearing: nobody else. He got her under way; he brought her to anchorages. Unless the master was very ill or lost overboard, or a drunkard or otherwise obviously incompetent, then his watch-keeping mates had to learn his all-important job when promoted to it, for in a great many cases they had not been able to develop ship-handling skill at all. It could be different in smaller ships, of course, and for that reason wise youngsters from seafaring families always chose such vessels to learn their business. No brass-bound big-ships nonsense for them! But deepwater men were different.

To control a square-rigged ship, at sea or in port, in the various manoeuvres necessary to get her from A to B by making the best possible use of the available winds, was a complex and delicate art. The master of a square-rigger had to be as subtle as the conductor of an orchestra, and as precise as a surgeon. What was actually involved? There were two main manoeuvres that the master would control himself: trimming the yards for a change of wind, and putting the ship about.

Trimming the sails for a major change of wind was skilled work. The ship had to be kept going at her best speed in all conditions, and this was an art that could only be learned by experience over time. However, under real time conditions at sea, trimming had to be done quickly and correctly: any lapse or error would show at once in the ship's motion, the sound of the wind in the rigging, the smash of seas over her waist if it was bad, or a violent clumping at her bows which was the sound of rising seas smashing back at her as she smashed too heavily into them. A square-rigger had no over-drive. She could be moved at a certain optimum speed through the water, and the too-ambitious attempt to get more out of her than she had to give was more likely to drive her half-under. Trimming was a difficult business to do well, calling for plenty of experience and a nice 'flair'.

The greatest ordinary test for the novice master was putting her about, tacking or wearing her; and tacking was the more revealing. She did not throw herself swiftly across the wind's eye like a smart yacht, unless the conditions were perfect and she was a very well-designed ship in perfect trim. When you tacked a barque or a full-rigger, you had to throw her across the wind in the wind's face, getting her aback in the process of course, but too briefly (you hoped) to allow her to pick up sternway. It was essential to be both bold and precise, to choose the right moment, to let her swing but not to stop her. But how to know?

The ship's length and all her sails were in your face at your place of control. There were signs, plenty of them: you must know them instantly and act upon them. As you have stopped her way to perform the manoeuvre, she will not steer. You have to get those yards correctly braced. Just as she swings through the wind's eye, you shout *Mains'l haul!* sharp, loud, and distinctive. Weather braces are let go, and there is instantly a wild cacophony. The backed head yards push the bow round. The sails on main and mizzen being aback with the wind's pressure going with the bow's swing, swing happily round from the one tack to the other at the precise, proper moment, the sailors gathering in the slack of what a moment earlier were the weather braces, hand over hand. The canvas quietens in response to the discipline of the yards. She's coming round.

Let go and haul! This is the next order. All know exactly what they have to let go, what to haul, where to find instantly all the gear that will do the job. Braces sing through their blocks: the course yards creak: chain sheets rattle. *Avast heaving on the royal there! Well the t'gallant! Check the upper tops'ls! Get that main topmast stays'l-sheet over! Belay the main brace! Set up the force braces now, lads!*

A scamper of feet to where these pins are, in their habitual places on the bulwarks pin-rails: but no wild rush. All know exactly what to do and how to do it swiftly and surely. Get those head-yards round before they become restive. Watch there, at the helm. Ease all that helm you'd put on her: let her come nicely to the wind on the new tack. Shift over the jibs, all the fore-and-afters. Look to the main-sheet and tack, in order that the biggest driving sail may fill and sing at its work. Shift over the spanker! *Helmsman, bring her by-the-wind!* Just let that weather clew of the mizzen-royal lift.

And there she is, drawing properly on the new tack, by your own calm self-confidence, judgement and skill: and the grace that the Clydeside builders have designed in the shapely iron hull that is your ship.

'Wearing ship' was simpler and needed far less nicety of judgement and nerve, though still a goodly measure of both. That was a hard-weather manoeuvre, storm stuff. You ran the ship off and she rolled her guts out and yours while the mariners hauled round the yards – both watches of the crew, with the wind still abaft the sails; the cook looking to the fore course sheet outside his galley-door, taking care that some fool sea lolloping over the rail did not take him aboard, or even wet him. Cooks hated getting wet.[11]

Naturally these manoeuvres could not be completed without the assistance of at least one mate (and in bad weather both) who would act as the relay and enforcer of the master's intentions; but this was essentially a subordinate role, and most mates were only able to develop the flair necessary to get the best from a sailing ship once in command.

What were the mate's other duties, apart from assisting the master in sailing manoeuvres? The watch-keeping officer would supervise the steering, make sure that reliefs of helmsman and lookouts were properly carried out, keep up the ship's deck-log, and supervise the heaving of the other log, the ship's speed-measuring device. This was a primitive arrangement of chip, a marked length of ratline-stuff, and a small sand-glass. In addition the mate was responsible for the cargo stowage in a ship, and the second mate, when he was allowed to, might pay some attention to navigation. As was seen in the case of the *Riversdale*, all too often neither mate was allowed any access to navigational matters.

The master, in fact, was God on his ship; and he had not even a minor prophet to contend with. Apart from handling his ship personally in its more complicated manoeuvres, he ran the ship's accounts, acted as ship's doctor, disciplined the crew, supervised rations, kept the ship's official records, navigated, and, very often, as if all that were not enough, acted as agent and broker for his ship in port.

In the late nineteenth century most sailing ships, as has been mentioned before, were tramps. In those days, only large lines (like the Lochs, including the *Loch Etive*) which were in regular trades, kept their own agents in the larger ports they served. It was usual for sailing-ship masters to be business managers of their ship and her affairs, and they might even do a little trading on their own account. The *Otago* was a one-ship line, registered at Adelaide in South Australia. It may have occurred to Conrad that a dying master acting as his own business manager, with the ship, the voyage, the freights, everything, in his own hands, could leave affairs in a mess – an additional complication and problem for the new

11. For a full account of the sailing of a full-rigged ship, see Alan Villiers, *The Way of a Ship*. Hodder & Stoughton, London, 1953.

master, inexperienced in business as in command. To take over command in a well-run ship would be hard enough; the *Otago* would probably be a greater challenge still.

The coastal steamer came up the river into Bangkok, and Conrad had his first view of his new command. He was impressed by what he saw. He described the *Otago* later in *The Shadow-Line*, a partly autobiographical story written in 1915, as follows:

> At the first glance I saw that she was a high-class vessel, a harmonious creature in the lines of her fine body, in the proportioned tallness of her spars ... she looked like ... an Arab steed in a string of cart-horses. (*The Shadow-Line*, pages 60–61)

Indeed she was. Perfect in proportion, gracefully sheered, sweet of counter and fine of bow, her squared yards taut, trim, and seaman-like – here was a ship. Built in Glasgow in 1869, the *Otago* was 147 feet long, 26 feet wide, and had 14 feet depth of hull; but those bare details do not reveal the impression she conveyed. We can imagine that Captain Konrad Korzeniowski took a long look, absorbing the details, noting the *Otago's* perfect grace from her three trucks to her waterline; the stance of her masts; the grace of her sail plan (which his mind's eye would fill in upon the naked yards); the curve of her slim cutwater and the perfection of her counter – the whole adding up to as nice and graceful a little barque as he had seen. She should handle well, sail faithfully, swing across the wind before it or into its eye gracefully, and tack in an angel's breath without losing way.

Splendid: but there soon proved to be an absence of the Angelic Host in the ship's crew. The Arab steed's riding crew was a mixed lot indeed, led by a mate who resented the coming of the new master sent to take over from him, and who was very soon showing this in every way of which he could think. Moreover, the little barque's business affairs seemed to be in a wholehearted mess, as Conrad may have anticipated; and sickness among the crew was a complication.

The *Otago* was chartered to load a full cargo of teak logs in Bangkok and take them to Sydney. The logs were ready, and Conrad's first real task as master (apart from investigating the confusion in which Captain Snadden had left the *Otago's* financial affairs) was to get the logs aboard his ship. This would be aided by the ship's heavier tackles and an elephant or two on the wharf – large, industrious beasts with five working 'legs' which were even more efficient than the old Dobbin which had helped to hoist out the coal cargo of the *Skimmer of the Sea* at Lowestoft years before, and which was still probably employed at the same job.

The cargo stowed, the next step was its delivery four or five thousand miles away. How was the new master to make the passage? Which route should he choose, to make the best passage from Bangkok to Sydney? For a sailing ship, the best passage was not necessarily the shortest one on the chart. The sailing ship depended entirely on the wind for both propulsion and steerage, and had to make use of prevailing winds where available. She had also to avoid obvious hazards, such as dangerous reefs, shoals, and rocks. And she (or rather, her master) had to bear in mind that some charts were unreliable in any case, and that some at least of the ocean was simply uncharted. This was despite the efforts of the Royal Navy's department of hydrography in charting the oceans.

The great navigator Captain James Cook had been sent on his extraordinary voyages of discovery, during which he had encircled Antarctica, charted the coast of New Zealand and the east coast of Australia and become the greatest Pacific explorer of all time, at the behest of the Royal Navy and only a century before Conrad sailed the seas. Conrad had read of his exploits as a youth. Cook had learned his trade as a merchant seaman in the North Sea, sailing out of Whitby in Yorkshire.[12]

There were other square-rigged ships in port as well as Eastern craft. Conrad sought advice from the experienced old master of a Bremen ship alongside near the *Otago*'s berth, and other masters he met casually in chandlers' stores or the British Consulate. The old German had good data, though he had not made that passage himself. His fat old barque waddled between Eastern ports and Bremen, out and back again round Good Hope, 10,000 miles each way. This seemed about all he really knew.

No sailing-ship master could know all that might be known for all trades on the vital matter of enabling his owner's ship to be blown expeditiously from one port to another, thousands of miles away. In those waters, Conrad knew little or nothing on this subject. Such knowledge was not on British curricula for merchant seamen at any level. He had never been in the South China Sea except through the Sunda Straits twice, once in the *Palestine* and once again in the *Highland Forest*, and the *Palestine* had got very little further. The steamship *Vidar* traded direct to the east coast of Borneo and Celebes: this was no help at all. There were some charts aboard with various noon positions marked here and there from previous voyages, but these data were scattered and disorganised.

So what to do? There was a tug to tow sailing ships out of the placid river into the Gulf of Siam; and all seemed agreed that the best route thence was to make south for the Sunda Straits and get through these to the Indian Ocean, where the southeast trade wind would be relied upon, taken full-and-by just for'ard of the barque's port beam, to push her along to the south in good order. But, of course, that propulsion would be only through the zone of the trade wind, which was more or less confined to the tropics. After that she must do the best she could to reach the west-winds zone south of 40 degrees, and blow along to Bass Strait or the south of Tasmania ('running her easting down', as sailors called that wild gallop), then slip up the Tasman Sea (a squally place) and into Sydney. It could take fifty days, or a hundred. Calm was the curse, not excess of wind. You could shorten down in heavy winds, but with no wind there was nothing to do.

---

12. For a full account of the life and achievements of this remarkable navigator, see Alan Villiers, *Captain Cook, the Seaman's Seaman.* Hodder & Stoughton, London, 1967.

On 9 February 1888, after the urgent solution of various problems in the ship's business affairs and among her crew, and with her hold as full as possible of valuable teak logs, the *Otago* put to sea, dribbled a little on her way, and then sat there as if she thought this a good place to rest and meant to stay there perhaps for ever – a wretched prospect indeed!

Conrad knew from seamen's hearsay and passed-down yarns that a few square-rigged ships had dribbled into calm so prolonged and profound that they had made extremely long passages; and it was said that in some cases the depressed crews had taken to the boats and rowed away before they were finally out of food and water (in 1907 this actually occurred on a ship named the *Alexandria*). However, such yarns were mainly of the Sargasso Sea, where great masses of floating weed came into it: weed enough to stifle the sea, choke the ship, even to prevent the crew from rowing. But this was not the Sargasso Sea, and to the best of Conrad's knowledge they were only seamen's yarns anyway.

Conrad's first command was now providing more than enough challenges. He had a sick crew, a disgruntled mate, an uncertain business enterprise and, to cap it all, no wind! There is no doubt but that under these trying circumstances the new master acquitted himself extremely well. Calm could happen to anyone: it was an endemic problem on certain routes, at certain times of the year, in the old sailing-ship days. A master could retire to his cabin and play the violin, start to drink his way through his private stock of liquor, or do nothing at all, as he chose. Conrad did none of these things, but occupied himself with surveying the medicines (short on them), the stores, and whatever else he could get at, and reading carefully through the few old deck-logs left aboard to learn what he could from them about the *Otago*'s passages.

What he could not find was anything in the way of ship's accounts – a vital part of her voyaging. He had been informed that the *Otago* usually earned something on the side, in addition to the income from her regular charters fixed before beginning a voyage – short local trips in the China Seas and elsewhere. Many such small ships did that, and the master was the authorised business manager, earning a percentage on the deals he managed on his owners' behalf. Perhaps the previous master had mailed these accounts to Adelaide. As it happened, this was not the case. It was Captain Korzeniowski himself who sorted out the ship's accounts and sent them off to Adelaide. At Sydney a letter from Simpsons awaited him, thanking him for his work and saying:

> The accounts which you enclosed are no doubt all in order but I have no means of comparing them with other documents as the late Captain never favoured me with a scratch of the pen from the time of leaving Newcastle [NSW] in August last and the acting master, Mr Burns [Born] only wrote me a brief note acquainting me with his Captain's death. Therefore, I am at a loss to know what business was done by the ship after she arrived at Haiphong, whether she earned or whether she lost money. In fact, other than your documents, I have no record whatever of receipts and expenditure. Will you, therefore, please inform me whether any freight was obtained between Haiphong and Bangkok and if so, how much and generally what business was done by the ship for the ten months previous to your assuming command.

The calm did not unduly depress the crew. More days meant more dollars. But the shortage of medicines began to be serious. There had been cholera about at Bangkok, as well as other nastinesses: Conrad was fortunate to avoid infection. And still the days burned slowly by, with the barque as often motionless as not, or with the flat and limpid sea slowly gurgling at her cutwater as she very gently pitched just a little or rolled almost imperceptibly, as if she were trying to show, in that stifling heat and prevailing calm, that she still had some dim and distant memory of what her true role should be. This was an unwanted way of beginning a sea passage, of starting a first command, with a sick crew and a becalmed ship. It was as well that the new master was a patient man and a stable character.

Sometimes there would be idle flickers of wind – cat's-paws, which scarcely broke the dead surface of the sea, and hardly caused the square sails of the barque, hanging lifeless and flat like the sides of an old circus tent, to flap. And yet the new master noted with pleasure that the *Otago* drew steerage way from the flap of those same big sails, as if she were anxious to get along, to show what she could do. But for many days there was no proper sailing breeze, and the cat's-paws did not last long enough for the sails to be properly trimmed to them.

This was no use. The *Otago* left Bangkok with far too much sickness amongst her small crew, and she was bound a long way. Captain Korzeniowski decided that there was only one thing he could do. He must put into Singapore (more or less on his way, if the barque ever got going) and get his crew well again.

So the little *Otago* sailed slowly to anchorage in Singapore Roads on 1 March 1888, a sailing ship in distress, with three members of her small crew needing to go into hospital – although her only real ailment had been lack of wind, a standard condition in the Gulf of Siam at that time of the year. A lack of some elementary medicines had been no help. She had no damage apart from that to the health of her crew. Some of them had not been fit when she sailed, for the *Otago*'s voyage had included other trying ports and passages before Conrad joined.

Really, the little barque had not done too badly: despite the abundance of calm she had reached Singapore Roads only three weeks out from the Bangkok River, more or less dribbling the 800 miles. Many a big square-rigger took that long just to work herself through the doldrums of the great oceans.

Indeed, Conrad had shown himself to be a resolute and capable ship-handler, prepared to make use of whatever wind was available. At one point in his slow passage, trying to fight the ghastly calm, he had drifted close in under the land among the islands of Ko Chang, Ko Mak and Ko Kut in the northern part of the Gulf of Siam, expecting that at least there should be alternating land and sea breezes there with all that sun burning the sea's surface all day, and the forested land of the islands cooling the night air. But the winds had seemed too worn out by the day-long sun to work at all. There were some movements of air, not wind, and he got some way out of her, but the mate looked at him as if he was hazarding the ship in a frightening manner – indeed, almost as if he suspected the master meant to wreck her, or was out of his mind.

Highland Forest sighting ice

Otago running in a gale off Cape Leeuwin

Torrens becalmed in mid-Atlantic

HM 'Q' Ship *Ready* in the North Sea

Many deepwater sailing-ship officers hated to have the land – any land – nearer the ship than could be avoided. Conrad's move, however, was good seamanship, and it did help a little. Obviously he had no fear of the land, and his voyages in the *Vidar* had helped him there. Conrad reflected on this manoeuvre many years later:

> On our first leaving port (I don't see why I should make any secret of the fact that it was Bangkok) a bit of manoeuvring of mine amongst the islands of the Gulf of Siam had given him [the mate] an unforgettable scare. Ever since then he had nursed in secret a bitter idea of my utter recklessness. (*Mirror of the Sea*, page 19)

He was also to make use of this episode in his story *The Secret Sharer*. In this intriguing work of fiction, a ship's new master secretly takes aboard a distressed mariner who has killed a member of another ship's crew, hides him on board his own ship, and then sails recklessly close to land in order to give the secret sharer the chance to slip into the water, swim ashore, and make another life. This story has generated enormous interest, not least, perhaps, for the moral ambiguity on which it appears to rest; for the new ship's master is enabling another ship's officer to avoid arrest for the crime, at the least, of manslaughter.

There are mitigating circumstances. The killing is not premeditated, but occurs in the heat of the moment: the ship *Sephora* is in danger of loss in heavy weather and the reefed foresail must be set if she is to be saved.[13] Her petrified master fails to give the appropriate order and Leggatt, the capable and resolute young mate, takes matters into his own hands: not only the setting of the sail, but the throat of the sailor who obstructs him.

> We closed just as an awful sea made for the ship. All hands saw it coming and took to the rigging... It's clear I meant business, because I was holding him by the throat still when they picked us up. He was black in the face. It was too much for them. It seems they rushed us aft together gripped as we were, screaming 'Murder!' like a lot of lunatics, and broke into the cuddy. And the ship running for her life, touch and go all the time, any moment her last in a sea fit to turn your hair grey only a-looking at it. I understand that the skipper, too, started raving like the rest of them. (*The Secret Sharer*)

The young ship's captain, who is the narrator of the story, feels that he must help Leggatt to escape the legal consequences of his act, rather than to plead the circumstances in court as mitigation or extenuation. Leggatt (like Lord Jim) is the son of a parson, and does not wish to bring disgrace on his family. Rather than face a trial for murder (or manslaughter), he would rather die, or live the rest of his life in exile from civilisation – for no judge and jury could ever be brought to understand the reality of life and death at sea.

Conrad may have drawn part of his inspiration for *The Secret Sharer* not only from his service in the *Otago*, but also by learning of an episode that had taken place on the famous clipper *Cutty Sark* (now preserved in Greenwich, England). In 1880, Captain Wallace of the *Cutty Sark* set sail from Penarth in Wales for the East, laden with naval quality coal, a bullying mate called Smith, an inadequate second mate, and a small crew which included

---

13. A sail is reefed to reduce its surface area. Please see glossary for further explanation.

a superstitious old salt called Vanderdecken who acted as a sort of one-man Greek chorus in the tragedy that was to follow. The mate pushed his watch too hard, including a black steamer hand called Francis, and the two men came to blows because Francis refused to do his duty when trimming ship. The upshot was that the mate killed Francis with a capstan bar. As Alan Villiers tells the story:

> The ship was in an uproar. Francis dead was more trouble than Francis alive, and Vanderdecken stirred the hands to a state of undeclared mutiny. The mate locked himself in his cabin and Captain Wallace took his watch.[14]

Wallace foolishly allowed Smith to escape the ship when at anchor in Anjer, and the mutiny became an open one. Wallace at once began to sail the ship with the apprentices and petty officers. But as soon as she entered the Java Sea she ran into an absolute calm. Calm is the great curse of sailing ships, and poor Wallace showed the strain dreadfully. After four days, he walked over the side. A boat was lowered, but nothing was seen of him again. Almost at once, a faint breath of air got up. The second mate took the ship back to Anjer and cabled the owner for advice, rather than seizing the opportunity and completing the voyage under his own command.

Years later, Sydney Smith was brought to trial at the Old Bailey for the wilful murder of John Francis. He is said to have been recognised by Vanderdecken. He was convicted of manslaughter and sentenced to seven years' penal servitude, served his time, returned to sea, worked his way up to ship's officer once again, and died in 1922 aged 73.

All this was far ahead of Captain Korzeniowski of the *Otago* as he shipped what amounted to a new crew in Singapore, and prepared for the voyage to Sydney. This was sure to be a very different type of passage from that from Bangkok to Singapore. The new leg of the voyage led to the Straits of Sunda and then into the great breadth of the Indian Ocean, where the wind had plenty of play. The course would be due south, or as near that as the *Otago* could manage with the faithful trade winds of the Indian Ocean on or just ahead of her port beam; and then a long curve eastwards somewhere round 36–40 degrees south, to pick up those brave west winds down there, blow the stagnant air out of her, and let her go!

To drive a responsive, well-behaved square-rigger making her easting in that part of the Southern Ocean that seamen knew as the 'Roaring Forties' was a challenging and invigorating business, in a well-run and well-maintained ship – stimulating for all aboard, but above all for the master. The *Otago*'s heavy cargo gave her a good grip of the sea, yet she was not so heavily laden that she wallowed with every huge crest breaking over her as

14. Alan Villiers' account of this episode is to be found in *The Cutty Sark* (Hodder & Stoughton, London, 1953), and is also published in *The Way of a Ship* (Hodder & Stoughton, 1953). He drew upon Basil Lubbock's *The Log of the Cutty Sark* (James Brown & Son, Glasgow, 1925).

if she were a wandering rock. Those teak logs were massive, bulky tree-trunks; she was far from full of them well before she was over her loaded draft, and no more could be carried. This trim kept her lively, saved her from rolling her guts out, as the uncouth seamen said, and gave the sweet hull good lift in the seas as she rolled along, taking those long, wet and breaking, tremendous jumps, jump after jump after jump – four thousand miles of them, with the wind roaring, and the spume and sprays flying!

The young Captain Korzeniowski had been in ships running their easting down before – in the Scots *Loch Etive* right around the rim of the southern world, and in the old, worn-out clipper the *Duke of Sutherland* – south of Good Hope towards Australia, homewards round the Horn. These were the elastic sailing-ship runs that meant a circumnavigation of the windy bottom of the world every voyage. He described crossing the Great Australian Bight as follows:

> It was a hard, long gale, grey clouds and green sea, heavy weather undoubtedly, but still what a sailor would call manageable. Under two lower topsails and a reefed foresail the barque seemed to race with a long, steady sea that did not becalm her in the troughs. The solemn thundering combers caught up with her from astern, passed her with a fierce boiling up of foam level with the bulwarks, swept on ahead with a swish and a roar; and the little vessel, dipping her jib-boom into the tumbling froth, would go running in a smooth glassy hollow, a deep valley between two ridges of the sea, hiding the horizon ahead and astern. *(Mirror of the Sea, page 75)*

'Arrived: May 7. *Otago*, barque, 367 tons. Captain Konkorzeniowski, from Bangkok: 68 days.' So the *Sydney Morning Herald* stated in its issue of 8 May 1888, offering the probably uninterested inhabitants of that city yet another of the many abortions of Conrad's comparatively simple Polish name, which were to appear in print from then onwards for years. (In Singapore he had been Korgormouski, which was not really trying at all.) Conrad's master mariner's certificate was issued under the name of Korzeniowski. He changed his name to Conrad, and saved himself a great deal of foolish trouble, only when his first book, *Almayer's Folly*, was published in 1895.

The *Otago* discharged part of her cargo of logs in Sydney and the remainder in Melbourne. She then loaded 2,750 bags of wheat and returned to Sydney. Sydney was the distant port where Conrad spent more time than any other (many months in the *Duke of Sutherland*, more in the *Loch Etive*). Previously he had had plenty of time to explore the place, but as a ship-master life was very different. There was always some matter of ship's business to be looked after. The *Otago* was then an Australian ship, and the owners in South Australia had reason to be pleased with their new captain's handling of his first command, including business matters.

She was chartered next to sail to Mauritius for a sugar cargo. Both Sydney and Melbourne were then more or less boom towns, with growing populations. There was a big demand for sugar, but as yet little local production. Some sugar was produced in Queensland to the north, with 'recruited' (i.e. impressed, or in effect enslaved) Kanaka labour, Polynesians brought in on contract from the islands, in some cases unscrupulously – but it was not enough to satisfy demand.[15] The nearest other source of sugar was Mauritius, where there was plenty of good sugar-cane, and excellent Indian labour (also brought by sailing ship). But to sail from Sydney to Mauritius presented problems as to the choice of a route for an engineless sailing ship.

It was one thing to sail from the Indian Ocean anywhere eastwards towards south or east Australia, for the oceanic winds on that route were reliably favourable. But it could be quite another matter for the square-rigger, large or small, to sail westwards from a port like Sydney back again. It was early May when the *Otago* reached Sydney – a winter month, when not only the Tasman Sea but the whole of the Great Australian Bight were notorious bad-weather areas. At that time of year, it might even have been better to make such a passage by boldly setting out eastwards towards the Horn to run with the westerlies round three-fourths of the world, rather than face the tough and sometimes terrible slog to wind'ard towards the west in a ballasted ship.

Square-riggers did not beat very well at the best of times, and some slovenly, wall-sided, barge-bowed sea-monsters were little use at all in trying to work to windward, especially in ballast, when with so much of the hull not immersed, they had much less grip on the water. A ship carried as much cargo and as little ballast as she could, for ballast and its loading and unloading was a cost and not a profit. Owners, who scrutinised all accounts, would try to ensure that the necessary minimum ballast to keep the ship upright was loaded, and no more. The sailing quality of the ship in ballast was a secondary consideration, if considered at all.

In 1919 the Scots barque *Garthneil* (later renamed the *Inverneil*) of over 1,000 tons had to take on the long eastwards Cape Horn route when bound merely from Melbourne towards Bunbury, Western Australia, to load railroad sleepers for the Cape railroad in Africa. She set sail from Melbourne on 6 July 1919, into gale-force westerlies. Although she made stout attempts to fight for those 2,000 miles west'ard and was a smart barque with a good crew, well commanded, she could not make it. Driven back without getting any reasonable distance at all, and not helped by being in ballast rather than cargo, Captain Shippen put in for shelter in Sydney on 29 July 1919. He tried again but again faced unfavourable winds, consulted with his first officer – and set out to go the other way, round Cape Horn. He kept his charter by sailing round the whole southern hemisphere except for the distance westwards from Melbourne to Bunbury, which they reached 76 days out from Sydney. The ship had sailed 14,563 miles in total, at an average speed of 191.6 miles per day, and Captain Shippen was able to calculate that, given the prevailing winds at the time, to have attempted to sail directly to Bunbury would have taken him much longer.

---

15 See Alan Villiers, *The Coral Sea*. Museum Press, London, 1949. Further details may also be found at the end of this chapter.

Conrad had loaded cargo and not ballast, and it would have been quite wasteful and even stupid to have taken the *Otago* to Mauritius either eastwards round most of the world, or westwards (and *below* Australia, as it were), slogging her into a succession of westerlies, with the sea drifts and current also against him, when there was another possibility. There was a better way for handier, smaller ships to go, and that was to get away from Sydney with a good southerly wind and drive her north as fast as possible, up to the Torres Strait north of Australia, slip through that potentially dangerous thoroughfare with appropriate caution, and simply keep going past all northern Australia, to let her romp merrily over the Indian Ocean before the splendid southeast trade wind until she reached Mauritius, out in the Indian Ocean to the east of Madagascar.

This was in fact the recommended route, although with the somewhat low standard of navigation and pilotage then (and later) in many big sailing ships, the majority of masters did not take it on. It was officially recommended, and many of the handier square-riggers sailed successfully that way before and after Conrad's time. Coolie-carriers travelled north-about Australia bound back to India or to Mauritius from Fijian ports. Big square-riggers sailing down from San Francisco or Puget Sound bound for Fremantle or Bunbury, or any of those ports, took the northern route also. It was the sensible route for them.

So Captain Korzeniowski took the *Otago* that way too, being a sensible and competent sailing-ship seaman acting in his owners' interests (to say nothing of his own and his crew's), and he made a nice fair-winds romp of it. It was only long afterwards, that the myth of this as a most unusual and daring way to go, an extraordinary piece of sailing, began to circulate. Captain Korzeniowski (like writer Joseph Conrad) knew what he was doing in ships, whatever he took on. He may not have sailed that way himself, but he had read of the voyages of Captain Cook when a boy in Russia and Poland. Where Cook had sailed, he could follow.

According to his own record, Conrad sought the permission of his owners to take this passage, rather than attempt to beat westwards against the prevailing westerlies, or sail the other way, right around the world. Perhaps surprisingly, although it was the longer option and attracted a higher insurance rate, they agreed. As Conrad described the projected voyage when he later wrote of it, he may have contributed to the myth that came to surround it:

> All of a sudden, all the deep-lying historic sense of the exploring ventures in the Pacific surged to the surface of my being. Almost without reflection I sat down and wrote a letter to my owners suggesting that, instead of the usual southern route, I should take the ship to Mauritius by way of Torres Strait. I ought to have received a severe rap on the knuckles, if only for wasting their time in submitting such an unheard of proposition. (*Last Essays*, page 26)

In reality, the supposedly excessive danger of this Coral Sea–Torres Strait route, the north-about route between eastern Australian ports and the Dutch East Indies or Mauritius, was greatly exaggerated. There was no need to sail north *inside* the Great Barrier Reef, which would certainly have been risky. It was better to sail outside, not just for avoidance of coral patches, but for better wind. That reef area, on the whole, was well defined. Beyond it to the east the so-called Coral Sea was reasonably free of dangers, considering the fine weather and good visibility prevailing there much of the year. There *were* reefs in the Coral Sea itself, of course – plenty of them, many unmarked by man, but all well indicated in the sea by nature's own excellent arrangements, with breakers noisily smashing over the shallower patches (they can be heard from miles away in quiet sailing ships) and the light of the great growths of coral changing the colour of the sea and, above the larger growths, of the daylight sky.

By day, with a lookout aloft in the main and fore crosstrees, one could see the evidence of reefs far off; by night they could be heard, for the ship was silent. There was no doubt about them in the usually prevalent good weather. The Coral Sea, like the Indian Ocean in the Mauritius area, was subject to a cyclone season, and 'cyclone' here is another name for hurricane. As Alan Villiers wrote when researching this passage: if these words on a weather chart scare you, better not take a big square-rigger to sea at all.

Alan Villiers sailed the full-rigged ship *Joseph Conrad* to the nor'ard through the Coral Sea with a fair wind, then had to beat her out again from far down in the leeward corner, towards the Roaring Forties and, in due course, Cape Horn.[16] She was a single-tops'l ship, much more of a handful than the modern-rigged *Otago*. He was not in the area by chance: Captain Villiers was bound first to the Louisiades and the Trobriand Islands, and thereafter towards New York. It took time, but he made it. After all, Tasman, Cook, Bligh and Flinders had all come through the Torres Strait by guidance of their eyes, ears, and the ship lead-lines alone.

That north-about route from Melbourne or Sydney was used by 3,000-ton four-masted barques in the Australian grain trade as late as the 1930s. They had no engines and were manned mainly by boys rather than men. The Swedish *C. B. Pedersen* was one which did this – inadvertently giving one young seaman the chance to jump ship and swim ashore to a coral island that appealed to his imagination, giving the ship no option but to sail on and leave him.

So Conrad chose the north-about route, and made a success of it. Conrad sailed from Sydney on 7 August 1888, leaving against advice in a heavy southeasterly gale. On arrival at the entrance to the Torres Strait, he took the Prince of Wales Channel, the best passage through, with fewer of the hazards of rapid and uncertain tidal streams than the more northerly passages. Midway though the Torres Strait Conrad brought the *Otago* to anchor at Thursday Island, where she lay for nine hours, awaiting a favourable tide; otherwise, the passage was without incident. Captain Korzeniowski had clearly heeded whatever

16. Alan Villiers, *Cruise of the Conrad*. Hodder & Stoughton, London, 1937. Republished by Seafarer Books, Rendlesham, 2006.

advice was available at the time. A later source offers advice as follows:

> Of the several channels through Torres Strait, Prince of Wales channel is the best. As in the passages northward of Prince of Wales channel the tidal streams are rapid and uncertain, and there are few marks to lead clear of the numerous dangers in them, it is strongly recommended that no vessel should attempt to pass through Yule, Bramble, Banks or Bligh channel, either from eastward or westward, without first anchoring and sending boats to mark the sunken dangers at the western entrances; even with this precaution, and the aid of the chart, a most vigilant look-out from the masthead is necessary and in no case should the attempt be made with the sun ahead.
>
> The rates [of tidal streams] predicted for Prince of Wales channel can be regarded as about the greatest likely to be experienced in any channel normally used for navigation. Constant attention must be paid to the vessel's position when approaching Prince of Wales channel. (1950 *Australia Pilot*, Vol. III, published by the Admiralty)

Overall, it was a good passage. No-one jumped overboard from the *Otago*, which made Mauritius on 30 September 1888, 54 days out from Sydney after a safe and pleasant passage with good wind almost all the way: this was indeed an excellent route at the right time of the year. It was wholly south of the equator, and the southeast trade wind was favourable for the *Otago* in the Indian Ocean too, blowing the little ship pleasantly right to the port for which she was bound. What a splendid experience for the young Polish master, and what a feat too!

The old barque had not lost as much as a rope-yarn, and the crew from master to youngest lad were probably darker-tanned and fitter than they had ever been before. The north-about passage was a glorious tropic holiday with quiet and peace and pleasant progress – day after day, week after week of splendid sailing with the flying fish startled by the roll of foam at the foot of her cutwater, taking off gracefully at the bow, and the gentle wake softly bubbling in the sunlight astern.

At Mauritius she had to discharge her cargo, line the hold to stow the sacks of sugar to take its place, and slip out again to sea – this time bound back towards Australia south-about, by way of the Roaring Forties. On the face of it, Conrad appears to have enjoyed his relatively brief stay in Mauritius, where the official language was French, and there was a well-established colonial society. There was something of the dandy about Conrad as ship-master: to go ashore he turned himself out very smartly, sporting a black or grey bowler and gloves, as well as carrying a cane with a gold knob. The other ship-masters, noting his fastidiousness in appearance and dress, polished manners, and pronounced foreign accent (in English at any rate, for his spoken French was better) nicknamed him the Russian Count. For a man born to Polish victims of the Russian empire, this was irony indeed.

Port Louis may have reminded the now successful Conrad of his first seafaring days in Marseille. It certainly gave him the opportunity to mix with people other than seafarers or lodging-house keepers – including the fairer members of the opposite sex. He described Mauritian society members later on in a short novel called *A Smile of Fortune* as, although of noble origin, impoverished, and 'living a narrow domestic life in a dull, dignified decay.' The girls are 'almost always pretty, ignorant of the world, kind and agreeable and generally bilingual: they prattle innocently in French and English. The emptiness of their existence passes belief.'

However, these somewhat unkind remarks may have been tinged by a forced disenchantment. As a young ship's captain of 30, Conrad would have been fascinated by Mauritian society, and he proposed marriage to one young beauty, a mademoiselle Eugenie Renouf – only to learn that she was engaged to be married to a local chemist, a fact of which she had somehow previously failed to inform him.

Another ship's officer might have laughed this off, or at least set it down to experience; but not Conrad, whose boyhood and choice of profession (which gave him a great deal of time on his own, whether at sea or in port, awaiting another cargo) had established in him a habit of introspective brooding which coloured his entire outlook. He took deep offence, returned to his ship, and swore never to return to Mauritius.

The *Otago* sailed from Mauritius on 22 November 1888 and reached Melbourne 44 days later, on 5 January 1889. She went on to make at least two brief coastal passages in Australian waters while Conrad was in command. Perhaps Conrad did not care for the short trips, for on one at least – from a Spencer Gulf outport to Adelaide – the barque was virtually a sailing lighter moving a few hundred tons of grain. The truth was that she was small for deep-sea runs, but this was no real employment for an efficient square-rigged ship. Conrad seems to have made good friends at both ends of the very short turn. Pleasant memories of him survived in South Australia, and he might have settled there happily enough. But his roots were still deep in Europe.

Simpson and Sons refused his request for more adventurous voyages, and accepted a charter to sail again to Port Louis, capital of Mauritius, and home of Eugenie Renouf and her gossiping friends. Rather than go, Conrad resigned his command, for he had determined never to return to the scene of his humiliation in Port Louis. Perhaps this was a sign that he had not entirely outgrown those Korzeniowski family characteristics of impulsiveness and recklessness of which his uncle had been so critical. Perhaps he had simply outgrown the *Otago*: she was a small ship with a small crew, and the only other officer on board was the mate, Born – who was hardly congenial company. (Born, although obtaining his master's certificate in Melbourne, was not appointed to succeed Conrad in command.)

On 26 March 1889, Conrad signed off the articles of the 'dear old *Otago*' and within a week or two was on his way as a passenger by liner to England. His useful salary in the *Otago* had allowed him to save the money for the fare, and he was frugal, at least when at sea; he had something over for expenses.

No berth that attracted him offered when he reached London; but perhaps he did not look very hard. He had absorbed a great deal from his eastern experiences, and his first command. One day in 1889, instead of reading a book after breakfast in his lodgings, he began to write. He worked on a story that he was to call *Almayer's Folly*. It was set in the East. It seems that he was trying his hand – but he was by no means finished with the sea yet.

Sugar, trade and forced labour: the blackbirders

In his carefully researched *The Coral Sea*,[17] Alan Villiers wrote of the background to the importation of sugar to Australia, long before he decided to write a biography of the sea career of Joseph Conrad. The story is both fascinating and horrifying, and would have been of extraordinary interest to Conrad, especially as he was to encounter and describe unabashed slavery in the Congo, a subject to be addressed in a later chapter.

Nineteenth-century Australia was an empty country and needed labour. European migrants were expensive and sometimes hard to get, and there were easier sources of manpower closer to hand, in what Australians called 'the Islands', i.e. the islands of the South Pacific. The natives there were known as blackbirds, and the people who ensnared them to work on the Queensland sugar-cane plantations, as blackbirders.

Blackbirders came in two sorts, although in practice the distinction sometimes meant very little: those who were licensed to recruit native labour in the South Pacific, and those who were not. The latter were out-and-out robbers; the former disguised their activities with a very thin veneer of legality. Both tricked potential labourers into going on board, if they did not kidnap them outright. How did they do so? As Villiers wrote:

> Another favourite means of ensnaring blackbirds was to carry a decoy. This was a native who pretended he was a prosperous ex-plantation worker. It was his duty to tell tales, to all who would listen, about the delights of working in Queensland and the easy fortunes who awaited the Melanesian there ... This kind of trick usually sufficed only once, now matter how well done. News moved fast by the bush telegraph, and still does. The blackbirder had to think of some new scheme almost every voyage. It was simplest, in the long run, to concentrate on plain kidnapping, or pay a strong chief to provide the bodies.

Slave labour, in effect, was therefore being used in a British colony, and it was not so very different from what was occurring in the Belgian Congo at the time. In *Heart of Darkness* Conrad wrote of the savagery with which the native inhabitants there were treated by their colonial overseers, and he said that he went only a little way beyond reality. But what, meanwhile, of what was happening in Queensland? Was the enslavement of Pacific islanders quietly tolerated? Or was some effort made to address the issue?

Indeed, such an effort was being made, and by no less an organisation than the Royal Navy, for the whole of the nineteenth century by far the largest navy in the world, and well used to dealing with slavers. As Alan Villiers reports, however, the pretence of legality in Australian waters could sometimes make naval action difficult:

---

17. Alan Villiers, *The Coral Sea*. Museum Press, London, 1949.

In an ocean where white men, well known to be murderers of natives and active slave traders, could carry on as they liked, the few naval vessels on patrol could hardly be expected to cope with all evils. Even when they caught slavers red-handed, it was almost impossible to secure a conviction against them in the courts of New South Wales ...

On several occasions British men-o'-war brought recruiters and their ships into Sydney and forced notorious slavers to stand trial. There are few records of successful prosecutions. 'I would like to be informed what constitutes the definition of a slave in these waters,' said Commander Palmer of HMS *Rosario* when the desperadoes of the hell ship *Daphne* walked smiling out of the Sydney courts, after facing charges that almost anywhere else would have hanged them. Commander Palmer added that if the African slave trade had been conducted in accordance with the precepts of the courts of New South Wales, it would still be a flourishing industry.

The *Daphne* was a schooner of less than 50 tons, registered in Melbourne and commanded by one Daggett, said to be a native of Boston, Massachusetts. The schooner was licensed as a recruiting vessel in accordance with the laws of the colony of Queensland and was authorised to carry not more than 58 native labourers. One day in 1869 Daggett sailed into Levuka Roads in the Fijis with more than 100 Banks Islanders clapped down below. His only papers were a clearance from Australia towards to the New Hebrides. At anchor off Levuka was HMS *Rosario*. Investigation showed the naval captain, who was no novice in these matters, that the *Daphne* was fitted out precisely in the manner of a West African slaver, except that she had no leg-irons. No interpreter was provided for the natives, who had no idea where they were or for what purpose they had been forcibly removed from their own islands ... The case was one of bare-faced slavery ... [but] was dismissed for 'lack of evidence'.

The remains of the *Otago*

Some ships, it would appear, never die. The *Otago* is a case in point, for although Conrad believed she had perished in his lifetime, her remains lie on a beach in the Derwent River near Hobart, Tasmania, to this day. The part-demolished hull of this iron barque has lain there since 1931, when the hulk was advertised for sale in the *Mercury*, a Hobart newspaper for which Alan Villiers worked as a young and rising reporter in an interval from the sea. She had been a coal hulk since 1903. Two attempts were made to demolish her for scrap in 1937 and 1961, but the old iron hull has so far proved indestructible, whether by man or tide and weather.

Her wheel is now the property of the Honourable Company of Master Mariners and is preserved on board the Company's headquarters ship *Wellington*, on London's Embankment. The *Otago*'s counter is currently in San Francisco in the keeping of the National Park Service, and the stem is reported to be in a museum in Turin. Finally, the teak companionway to the master's saloon which Conrad once admired for its excellent, simple taste has now been restored to its full magnificence and is on display at the Maritime Museum of Tasmania in Hobart.

Torrens

Conrad dabbled in business affairs, continued to work on *Almayer's Folly*, and looked for a suitable command. This he was unable to find. His thoughts then turned to Africa, which may have been the resurgence of a boyhood wish to explore the dark and mysterious corners of the earth. Conrad stated that when he was a youth he pointed to the blank space on a map of the interior of Africa and 'said to myself with absolute assurance and an amazing audacity which are no longer in my character now: "When I grow up I shall go *there*." ' (*A Personal Record*, page 13). Many children might voice such ambitions, but never put them into practice. Conrad did so.

Conrad needed to take some pains to further his desire, for going to the Congo, like becoming a ship's officer in the merchant navy, was not a straightforward ambition, easily achieved: there were obstacles in the way. He had no experience of Africa; he had no experience of navigating the Congo (or any other major inland water); and he had no connections with any Belgian commercial institutions. How was he to overcome them?

Conrad did what his uncle had done in securing him an opportunity to find out what it was like to go to sea, long ago in Marseille. He corresponded with a company in Brussels, using a relative's influence to good effect. The person in question was Marguerite Poradowska, a beautiful and sophisticated relative by marriage, a woman of strongly cultivated literary tastes who shared his passion for French literature, and with whom he launched a lasting correspondence: for the introverted Pole and the cultivated Frenchwoman (she was Polish only by marriage) had much in common.

He had originally corresponded with her husband, Mr Poradowski, but he died before the two men were able to meet in Brussels. His widow then advanced Conrad's claim. Did he ever wish to make her Marguerite Korzeniowska? There is no evidence that he did, for Conrad was a man who played most of his cards very close to his chest – but their relationship, if mainly an epistolary one, did allow Conrad to express his innermost self in a way that he was unwilling to do with others. His uncle may have scented that something was in the wind, for he warned his nephew not to sail too close to the beguiling if dangerous widow.

Conrad pursued his Congolese ambitions, and was eventually appointed to command a paddle-steamer on the Congo, based at Kinshasa. Conrad signed a contract to make the lengthy and difficult journey to the Congo on the understanding that he would be given the opportunity to understudy an existing captain once there and then command his own steamer. His contract required three years' service.

It was the last place on earth where one might expect a deepwater sailing-ship sailor to go. The Congo was a traffic-river, a watery highway in a most difficult terrain, cutting deep into a rich and still very much unknown continent. It had some stern-wheelers and other craft operating on it, all highly specialised vessels calling for detailed knowledge not only of their own handling, but also of every aspect of their pilotage. For great rivers are often intractable waterways, flowing rapidly through gorges and slowly in valleys, at times torrents, at times apparently placid: but always hostile, liable to flood or to dry out (at least in parts) – requiring, indeed, a degree of intimate personal knowledge of their ways, their range of beds, banks, shallows and other impediments and their dangerous idiosyncrasies, such as is utterly foreign to the deepwater seaman's whole experience. Among such rivers as the Brahmaputra, the Irrawaddy, the Amazon and the Mississippi (on which Mark Twain was once a pilot), the Congo is notoriously the worst of all.

If Conrad had wished only to have some river experience, both the Brahmaputra and the Irrawaddy were available to British merchant-service officers then, with the British India Company in Calcutta or the famous Irrawaddy Flotilla Company in Burma. But, and not for the first time, Conrad chose the right ship, the right background, and the right tragedy for his great talents.

Over a wandering life, Alan Villiers gained some experience of navigating great rivers, chiefly the Brahmaputra during the Second World War. He learned to have infinite respect for their power, strength, and obscure idiosyncrasies, and the absolute need to learn thoroughly about them and their ways before taking any of them on, in any sort of vessel. But he learned also to have an even greater respect for that wonderfully gifted man, Joseph Conrad.

It was one thing to dream about the Congo – hot, wet, and mysterious – when he was a boy in exile in cold and snow-laden Russia; but it was a very different thing for a grown man, a qualified and experienced blue-water sailor, actually to go to the Congo and take over command of a river boat, if only for a short period. This was a most extraordinary achievement, even for such a person as Conrad.

Conrad was engaged to spend three years in the Congo, and first had to reach Kinshasa, where he had been promised a command. He left Bordeaux on a French steamship in May 1890 and arrived at Bomo, 60 miles upriver from the mouth of the Congo, a month later. Travelling on by another vessel to Matadi, 30 miles further upriver, Conrad spent a fortnight there, and then made an overland trek of about 200 miles to Kinshasa on Stanley Pool, where small steamers that had been carried by section were assembled for further exploration of the mighty river Congo and its tributaries.

When he finally arrived at Kinshasa on 1 August 1890 there was no steamer for Conrad to command: it had been wrecked. Three days later Conrad joined the river steamer *Roi des Belges* to understudy its captain on the voyage to Stanley Falls, which they reached on 1 September. By this time the captain was sick, like most white men in the Congo, and

Conrad, although also ill with fever and dysentery, took command of the *Roi* for the return trip to Stanley Pool (Kinshasa) which was reached 18 days later on 24 September.

By this stage, Conrad was both physically ill and psychologically disillusioned – and had fallen out with the company directors, who failed to fulfil any promises that had been made to him. He was offered neither a steamer to command, nor the prospect of one in the near future. The Congo was extremely hot; conditions were squalid; disease was rampant. But much more upsetting was the moral atmosphere of the Belgian Congo, an atmosphere of naked greed and cynical exploitation and ruthless disregard for the oppressed. In Europe the Belgians presented the exploration and development of their new colony as a crusade. The reality was very different, as Conrad saw and went on to write about in *Heart of Darkness*. He found the company's local directors, and indeed nearly all the white men he met in the Congo, profoundly unsympathetic. The exception was his encounter with the anti-slavery campaigner Roger Casement, with whom Conrad shared accommodation whilst waiting to proceed overland from Matadi. In his way, Roger Casement was as unusual a person as Joseph Conrad. He died in disgrace, a traitor hanged by the British in 1916 for conspiring with the Germans – but before that official disgrace he had received worldwide admiration.

Roger Casement was born in Dublin in 1864 and joined the British consular service as a young man. He gained international renown for his consular reports highlighting and denouncing the appalling treatment of native workers in the Congo and Amazon areas. One was a Belgian colony (actually, the property of the King of the Belgians, rather than the Belgian state) and the other an independent nation, formerly a Portuguese colony, but the treatment of native labour was in both cases abysmal. In contemporary terms, it would have been called a wholesale violation of their most fundamental human rights. Casement was knighted for his services in 1911, retired from the consular service through ill health, and based himself once again in his native city of Dublin – where he became involved in the Irish nationalist movement, and helped to form the Irish Volunteers.

The son of a protestant father and Catholic mother, Casement may have had a natural sympathy for the underdog, and as in the Congo, he put his sympathies into action. Like another Anglo-Irishman, Erskine Childers,[18] who had previously rendered loyal service to the Crown, Casement embraced the cause of Irish independence not only as a matter of idealism, but by putting his own life at risk. On 12 April 1916 he was landed by German submarine near Tralee in Ireland. He may have intended to help promote the Irish uprising which was then planned. Or he might have intended to inform its leaders that they could not, in fact, expect any help from Germany at that time. Whichever the case, Casement's activities were soon ended, for on 24 April he was arrested by the British, taken to London, charged with and convicted of treason, and hanged on 3 August 1916. His defence was hampered by what would now be called a spoiling campaign: the circulation of his

18. See Erskine Childers, *The Riddle of the Sands*. First published 1903; republished by Seafarer Books, 1998.

homosexual diaries within official circles. In 1966 Casement's remains were returned to Dublin and given a state funeral.

Did the two subjects of imperialism, the Irishman and the Pole, talk politics together? We do not know, but it is clear that they achieved some sort of rapport. Conrad recorded in his diary at the time that Casement 'thinks, speaks well, [and is] most intelligent and very sympathetic'.

Conrad was to attack imperialism in his own way, through the medium of fiction. As a Pole, he was instinctively opposed to the oppressive actions of major powers such as Russia who rode roughshod over the dignity and self-respect of smaller nations. At the same time, however, Conrad was a cautious and complex person, whose beliefs were wrapped in a sort of circumspect cloud which he rarely if ever dispelled. He was conscious of his father's miserable fate as a patriotic idealist and rebel. He was conscious of the fact that he was a naturalised British subject, and it would be wise to avoid political controversy. Consequently, his attitude to revolutionaries – in which category we might include Sir Roger Casement, despite his highly 'establishment' consular service – was always ambivalent.

Finally, there is a sort of cynicism or rather pessimism about Conrad's political views, resting on a more profound cynicism about human nature itself. Conrad believed that human nature itself was flawed, and that political reform was therefore likely to be self-defeating. His plots tend to reflect this: they are pessimistic about people and their plans and usually end in failure. At best, there is a certain irony about Conrad's plots, but never, except in the heavily contrived *Chance*, what might be conventionally described as a happy ending, and the reverse is usually true.

The would-be riverboat captain Konrad Korzeniowski was sent home from the Congo on medical grounds, suffering from dysentery and malaria: the Congo shattered his health, and he was never the same afterwards. His short stay was not unusual: very few expatriates completed their three-year tour of duty in the service of the King of the Belgians. He returned to Europe on a steamer, to arrive back in London in January 1891 a sick man and an apparent failure, at least in material terms.

Spiritually, however, Conrad had gained from his visit to the Congo. He gained an insight into a very different world from that of the sailing ship, or of England, or of France or Poland, for that matter – an insight which is shown in *Heart of Darkness*, the story which he wrote based on his Congolese experiences, and in which, he said, he went only a little way past reality.

Conrad returned to England from the Congo in a state of very poor physical health and profound nervous depression. He was unable to work for some time; indeed, he would probably have had to pass up a command, were one offered. Then, after eight months' enforced sea-inactivity, he had a piece of very good luck: the master of the *Torrens* offered him the position of chief officer. This was a splendid antidote to the grabbing, murderous horror that the white man had made of the Congo.

The *Torrens* could justly be described as one of those few near-perfect ships in her own way, in a trade which perfectly suited her. She was what is called a 'composite' ship (stout wood planks on a strong iron frame, perhaps the best combination possible), built in Sunderland, England, in 1875, designed for the Australian trade – a superior sort of passenger carrier (no hold-jamming migrant cargo transport) though she had excellent cargo capacity as well. She was shapely, reasonably fast without being wet, and she handled very nicely – obviously a ship with a perfectly placed centre of effort in her well-planned sail area. She was about 1,200 tons register, an excellent size for a full-rigged ship – neither too big nor too small. She was, moreover, what a great many later-day 'windjammers' were certainly not – a 'nice' ship, almost as if she sailed with a benign spirit, a good-tempered ship somehow eager to do her best without hurting anybody, or herself.

She was built to behave well in the sea, and to last; never one of that large, bitchy breed of barrel-bowed sea-beasts which smashed into every sea in sight as soon as they were outside, as if eager to wash the wretched humans overboard and be done with them; the wallowing great hogs of the Roaring Forties, the sleepers in the doldrums, the slovenly beasts of the horse latitudes which never made any port from any other in less than 100 days. There were plenty of them, and they broke good seamen's hearts. Seamen used to call them 'windbags', never windjammers (a name which began with a sneer, too, but survived to indicate affection).

The full-rigged *Torrens* was neither windbag nor windjammer – nor sharp, wet-waisted alleged 'clipper'. She was a comfortable well-formed ship with burthen enough to ride dry in the sea, and lines good enough to slip along before a breath of air that would scarcely blow out a handheld match; lines which kept her reasonably 'dry' (used in the sailors' sense, not counting froth-like sprays and the tops of breaking seas that might blow over her) in anything short of full gale. Even better, the *Torrens* had good masters. To top it all, she was in the best run in the Australian trade: London to Adelaide and back. This meant that she sailed out and back again round Good Hope, with no Cape Horn. You might think of her almost as a rest-cure ship: her passengers certainly did.

She ran her easting down on the outward passage only, at a good clip once through the horse latitudes beyond the southeast trades, and she made the wide swing from the trades zone to the Roaring Forties in a useful area of the South Atlantic, noted neither for excessive calm nor for storm. Of course, she got her share of storm in the Forties: but this was 'easting-down' stuff, exhilarating, and glorious for running.

Homewards was generally even better. Instead of standing to the southeastwards and scuttling away in quest of the great west winds of the forties and fifties south – blustery, cold, trying latitudes at best – for the long, hard run towards the Horn, the Adelaide traders sailed westwards, for the winds in summer and the currents were in favour of square-rigged ships sailing homewards by way of the Cape of Good Hope. For this westbound route they crossed the Australian Bight first and, slipping past the elephant's foot called the Leeuwin at Australia's southwest corner, stayed in good weather and favouring currents to the tropic's edge and the southeast trades, for the several thousands of miles westing thence towards the friendly west-setting Agulhas current to help round the Cape of Good Hope – on the inshore side, no nonsense about fighting the Roaring Forties! No, indeed: and from the Cape, with a little luck, southerlies would waft you into the zone of the southeast trades – a flying-fish run the whole way. This was far better than the Horn, and the good *Torrens* regularly sailed that way. The ship might get a bit of a blow – a side-kick from a cyclone in the Mauritius area, perhaps – but the sea was warm and the wind too. What a glorious difference from that grim old Horn run!

Alan Villiers sailed that Good Hope way to Europe once, setting out from Melbourne in a big limejuice four-masted barque – a clodhopper named the *Bellands*, warehousing over 5,000 tons of Victorian grain in sacks, bound for Saint Nazaire. It was a flying-fish run almost from off the Leeuwin to the Bay of Biscay, nearly five months of it. It almost became trying for the monotony of the good weather.

Conrad stayed for two round voyages in the *Torrens*. He was mate aboard from November 1891, when the ship was some sixteen years old, until the end of July 1893, when she arrived back in London from the second voyage, 126 days out including a brief stop at Cape Town. Now Conrad left. The *Torrens* had more than served her purpose in his life, for the Roaring Forties and the sunny trade winds combined with the long, unhurried, and unworried wanderings of that splendid ship to restore him fully to at least as good health as he had ever known. He was to write of the *Torrens* with great affection in his *Last Essays*.

More than that, the ship was an unforeseen milestone in Conrad's literary career, for amongst the passengers carried from Australia to South Africa on his second voyage was John Galsworthy (not then a writer, but a young man just down from Cambridge, and supposed to be becoming a lawyer). Galsworthy later wrote of his initial impressions of Conrad, first as a seaman and secondly as a story-teller:

> He was a good seaman. Watchful of the weather, quick in handling the ship; considerate with the apprentices … With the crew he was popular; they were individuals to him, not a mere gang; and long after he would talk of this or that among them … Many evening watches in fine weather we spent on the poop. Ever the great teller of a tale, he had nearly twenty years of tales to tell … He was extraordinarily perceptive and receptive.[19]

Galsworthy was invited to Conrad's cabin for his last evening on the *Torrens*, and wrote 'I remember feeling that he outweighed for me all the other experiences of that voyage.'

Galsworthy and Conrad became friends for life, and this friendship was to be of great help to Conrad in his subsequent writing career. In the meantime, still on his first voyage on the *Torrens* and still working on *Almayer's Folly*, Conrad was confirmed

---

19. John Galsworthy, *Castles in Spain*. Heinemann, London, 1927, pages 74–76.

in his determination to continue with his experiment at writing by another passenger. In *A Personal Record* he describes how he offered the partially completed manuscript of *Almayer's Folly* to a young man called Jacques for his appreciation. Jacques read the manuscript, and returned it without a word.

> 'Well, what do you say?' I asked at last. 'Is it worth finishing?' This question expressed exactly the whole of my thoughts.
>
> 'Distinctly,' he answered. The purpose instilled into me by his simple and final 'distinctly' remained dormant, yet alive to await its opportunity. (*A Personal Record*, page 17)

Well might Conrad write of his experiences in the *Torrens* as having been 'most fortunate from every point of view, marking the end of my sea-life with pleasant memories, new impressions, and precious friendship' (*Last Essays*, page 22). In fact Conrad's days as a professional merchant-service officer were not quite finished; but he had reached a stage in life where he was becoming as interested in writing as in seafaring, and writing was soon to become his full-time occupation to the exclusion of the sea. The *Torrens* was the culmination of his sea-career. The *Otago* had been his first command, and he had acquitted himself extremely well; but in his two years as mate of the *Torrens*, a large, fast, and famous ship, he established beyond any doubt his pre-eminence in his sea-career.

Ready

In November 1893 Conrad was offered a post as second mate in the steamship *Adowa*, owned by the Franco-Canadian Transport Company: the ship was intended to carry migrants from France to Canada. In *A Personal Record* Conrad credits the Secretary of the London Shipmasters' Society, a Captain Froud, with obtaining him this post. However, the FCTC collapsed, and Conrad's service in the *Adowa* was limited to crossing the Channel from London to Rouen, and waiting there for a few weeks for the migrants who never came forward. Second mate in a steamship was hardly a promotion for the popular and successful first officer of the *Torrens*. Had the *Adowa* sailed, it would have been purely a fill-in job for Conrad. As things turned out, it was not even that, and Conrad returned jobless to London in January 1894.

Conrad's lack of a ship meant that at least he could devote his full attention to the manuscript of *Almayer's Folly*, his first novel, which he had begun writing in 1889 and had now been working on for five years. He completed the book in three months and submitted it to Fisher Unwin, a London publisher. After a delay of three months (and worry for Conrad: he was always an extremely anxious author, but in fact his first novel was appraised very quickly) it was accepted. Conrad was naturally extremely pleased. Unfortunately he could not share his joy with his uncle, who had supported and encouraged him in most of the other ventures of his life, for Tadeusz Bobrowski died in February 1894.

Almayer's Folly was published in April 1895, and Conrad received a total payment of £20. It met with an extraordinary critical acclaim for a first novel by a wholly unknown writer, but no popular success; and it certainly did not promise financial security to the new author. No matter: he was in print. He had obtained his first 'certificate' as an author, but he was not yet a master of this new craft. At this stage, Conrad still thought of himself as a professional seaman who wrote, rather than a writer who had sailed. He did not know if he had it in him to write another book, and he still intended to return to the sea, whose 'claims are simple and cannot be evaded' (*Chance*, 1913). However, although he did not realise or perhaps accept it for some time to come, his merchant-navy career was over.

Initially, he could not obtain a suitable command. He began to write another book, *An Outcast of the Islands*, based, like *Almayer's Folly*, in the exotic and mysterious Far East – exotic and mysterious to the ordinary British reader, that is, and thereby an excellent setting for popular fiction, although it was not until 1913 that Conrad's fiction achieved popularity, and he became known to a wider circle than that of the literary specialist. The apparent indifference of the ordinary reader to Conrad's output (wherever its setting) was a source of great anxiety to him. Not only did he need to make a living from his pen: he needed to know that what he wrote was reaching the broader public to whom he wished to appeal. Nevertheless, the life of an author became increasingly absorbing, as he became friendly with literary people – R. B. Cunningham Grahame, Ford Madox Ford and H. G. Wells amongst them – and gradually assumed the persona of the professional author towards which he had been unconsciously guided, perhaps, from early childhood.

In 1896 Conrad married Miss Jessie George, and thereby changed not only his marital status but also his way of life. For the first time since his early youth he began to live in a house rather than on board ship or in lodgings; and although the houses were rented, and the couple moved from one place to another in Sussex, Bedfordshire and Kent until finally settling near Canterbury, it was still a momentous change for the world-wandering Polish exile.

Conrad's proposal to the much younger Jessie was almost a caricature of the behaviour of the phlegmatic Englishman who might have been found in *Punch* at the time. 'Look here,' he is reported to have said to the young woman, after a period when he had taken her out, chaperoned, once or twice, but made no declaration of his intentions – 'Look here, my dear, we had better get married at once and get over to France.' (It was a wet and gloomy morning in February, and Conrad had chosen a seat in the National Gallery for this pier-head jump). 'How soon can you be ready? A week? A fortnight?' He further informed her that he did not expect to live for very long, and had no intention of having children – both of which prophecies proved incorrect. Altogether, it might have been a signing-on in a shipping hall, for all the apparent romance involved; and yet romance underlay it. She was the victim, and he the rescuer – although from what Jessie needed rescuing was not entirely clear.

His wife proved an invaluable support to the highly strung author, always prone to self-questioning and self-doubt, and a prey to various illnesses, both real and at least in part a result of his acute nervousness. Conrad wrote slowly and with extraordinary care, and his publishers (and later his agent) needed to exercise patience as well as offer financial support whilst he wrote his stories, many of which became much longer, and took much longer to complete, than he had originally intended. Jessie was calm and unflappable, an excellent cook and competent manageress of the Conrad household, who also typed and corrected his manuscripts. She became the mother of their two sons, Borys and John, in whom Conrad took a great pride.

Jessie was Conrad's anchor, and provided the element of stability that his life had always lacked; and in *The Mirror of the Sea* he declared the importance of the anchor to any ship. The Conrad marriage appears to have been a success, and not only because it survived. Some of Conrad's literary friends may have found her a bore, for Jessie had no artistic pretensions. Possibly there was an element of snobbery in their discrimination, for Jessie George came from a lower social background than the expatriate Pole and his artistic circle – with the significant exception of H. G. Wells, who was proud of his lower-middle-class origins. The Polish exile and the English typist, he partially crippled by gout and she by an accident to her knees which meant that she became increasingly heavy and immobile, were able to sustain, if not a meeting of minds, then a meeting of interests; and there may have been more to Jessie's insight into Conrad's mind than his literary friends realised.

Conrad's ambition to return to the sea gradually faded. At times he would express an interest in taking ship again, when he was particularly hard-up. Conrad was in financial difficulties for most of his life as an author, for financial success came very late, in the last nine years of his life. Similarly, he might express a yearning for the sea when the process of writing became especially tortuous: a sort of literary doldrums. But these were never serious sea-going plans: for writing absorbed him.

In 1896 Conrad travelled to Grangemouth in Scotland to inspect a small barque named the *Windermere*. She was a tough little three-master of 487 tons, about the same size as the *Skimmer of the Seas* or the *Otago*, and she was built in the composite style (wooden planks on a metal frame, like the *Torrens*.) She was laid up, and could have been bought cheaply through lack of bidders. Conrad took his wife-to-be Jessie with him on this trip, and both were horrified at the state of the *Windermere*, for she was in an utter mess: everything in her that was breakable had been broken, and the hull and decks were covered with a rich deposit of seagull droppings. The ship was abandoned, derelict, and dead. For Conrad, so sensitive to atmosphere, she could not be brought back to life. He made no bid for the *Windermere*. Eventually she was sold, and in 1900 lost at sea with all hands in the Channel. All seamen are superstitious, and perhaps, when Conrad read of her loss, a relief that he had avoided her may have been conjoined with his regret at her sad end.

Conrad was appalled by the catastrophe of the Great War and regretted his inability to participate in some active way in support of his adoptive country – although his older son was able to do so. In 1914 he was visiting Poland with his family when the advent of general war took them by surprise, and they had great difficulty in finding their way back to England though a war-torn and disrupted Europe. Conrad was determined to do something – somewhat ironically, it was at this stage of his writing career that his books had begun to sell, and his financial worries were reducing – and in 1916 he spent two weeks at sea on a naval 'Q' ship. She was a vessel actually named the *Ready*, but masquerading under the name of *Freya*, a sailing decoy-duck disguise to look like a defenceless merchant ship with a sort of barquentine rig. The idea was that a prowling German U boat would be tempted by the sitting duck and rise to sink her with its guns (thereby saving a valuable torpedo). Whereupon the *Freya* would change to the *Ready*, uncover a gun of its own, and sink the dumbfounded submarine. Ready she may have been, but so were the U boat commanders, and no U boat surfaced near the *Freya* whilst Conrad was on board – which is not to belittle his courage in shipping on the vessel in the first place.

The 'Q' sailing ship idea *was* used extremely effectively – but unfortunately by the Germans. Count Felix von Luckner, an officer in the Imperial German Navy who had previously sailed before the mast in a windjammer, captured and sank a large number of Allied ships, using an apparently innocuous sailing ship fitted with auxiliary engines: *and* did the whole thing with no loss of life, too. In later life, Alan Villiers met with Felix von Luckner, and the two became fast friends. Did he ever regret, the Australian asked the German, that he had sunk so many fine sailing ships? Of course he did, the German replied. And the reason? War, was the simple and unanswerable response.

Apart from his trip to look at the *Windermere*, and the occasional and very temporary urge to return to the sea, Conrad remained a former mariner, an expert on the sea, a man who took a close interest in maritime affairs, and who wrote articles on such incidents as the loss of the *Titanic* in 1912 – but from ashore. Conrad's writings about the loss of the *Titanic* (in *Notes on Life and Letters*, 1921, pages 287–334) show that his professional knowledge and insight was not confined to sail. No ship could be completely safe, wrote Conrad, in the course of making some highly pertinent remarks about how to design a comparatively safe ship, and the design of the Titanic was fundamentally flawed.

Her hull was divided into supposedly watertight compartments, to be sealed by a series of bulkheads in the event of a collision. However, those supposedly sealed compartments would not in reality keep her afloat in such circumstances, since the water would rise up each bulkhead in turn and overrun into the next section, until the ship sank. The only answer would have been to make each compartment *really* watertight, so that the bulkhead reached from keel to deck and formed a watertight seal. For the coal-hold, this would have to mean that the bulkhead rose from bottom to top, rather than top to bottom, for otherwise the coal lying on the ship's floor would prevent the bulkhead from descending. Conrad further commented that to design a ship so as to be apparently unsinkable would encourage perverse behaviour on the bridge, so that instead of attempting to avoid an obstacle such as another ship on a collision course, or an iceberg, the officer of the watch might be expected to ram it head-on, and rely on the ship's design to avert the full consequences of this counterintuitive action. Folly! Hubris! Disaster!

Perhaps when Conrad wrote of the loss of the *Titanic* he had in mind the circumstances of the *Patna* in his work of fiction *Lord Jim*, first published in 1900. The Jim in question was first officer on a steamship transporting Muslims to Mecca. The ship had sustained damage to her bows and the sea was pressing on the bulkhead behind them. Jim decided that the forward bulkhead could not withstand the pressure and shamefully joined the rest of the ship's crew in abandoning the ship to her fate, together with the hundreds of pilgrims on board. But the *Patna* survived and her deserters were disgraced, for the bulkhead kept out the sea after all. This story was based on a real episode at sea, the abandonment of the *Jeddah* in August 1880. As a serving merchant naval officer at the time, Conrad would have been fully aware of this incident; and the marine part of *Lord Jim* has an extraordinary vividness in its writing.

Conrad wrote of the sea in some (though far from all) of his works, but never again sailed as a ship's officer. He was reconciled to this in his absorption in writing. Nevertheless, there is a strong tinge of regret for things past and irrecoverable, in much of what he later wrote about his early days at sea. It is the essence of *Youth*. It permeates *The Mirror of the Sea* and *A Personal Record*, both semi-autobiographical reminiscences. And in the novel *Chance* Conrad describes the narrator, a middle-aged former seaman called Marlow, as follows (and the description would appear to fit Conrad himself as much as Marlow):

> Marlow had retired from the sea in a sort of half-hearted fashion some years ago. [But there was a] subtly provisional character [in] Marlow's long sojourn amongst us. From year to year he dwelt on land as a bird rests on the branch of a tree, so tense with the power of brusque flight into its true element that it is incomprehensible why it should sit still minute after minute. The sea is the sailor's true element, and Marlow, lingering on shore, was to me an object of incredulous commiseration like a bird which, secretly, should have lost its faith in the high virtue of flying. (*Chance*, page 53)

Conrad wrote about the sea in many of his books, and used the sea in others. It is notable that in his first great popular success, *Chance*, the Knight who saves the Maiden (these are Conrad's terms, and convey a certain detachment and irony) is a captain in the merchant navy with his own ship, of which he is inordinately fond. But *Chance* is not a tale of the sea as such, and the loss of Captain Roderick Anthony with his ship does not mean that the tale ends in tragedy. Indeed, it gives the second mate his chance.

Other books have little or no mention of the sea at all. *The Secret Agent* is set firmly on land, and although the main event of the story is an attempt by supposed anarchists to destroy the Greenwich Meridian, it would be stretching a point to insist that this lends a nautical flavour to the book. *Under Western Eyes* concerns anti-Tsarist conspiracy and its consequences in Russia, and has some similarities to Dostoyevsky's *Crime and Punishment* in its theme. Other stories, also, are set firmly on land.

Nevertheless, Conrad's nostalgia for the sea is both real and understandable. The sea gave Conrad the background and personalities he was to use in many of his stories. The sea moulded his character; it influenced his philosophy; it shaped his destiny. For the commander of the *Otago*, careful, patient, painstaking, and fully confident in his own judgement, was a very different person from the careless and extravagant young Pole who had arrived in Marseille to seek the patronage of the Delestangs so many years before. Conrad might have achieved the same maturity had he chosen some other career, but it seems doubtful. For, as he wrote in *Chance* (page 51):

> The exacting life of the sea has this advantage over the life of the earth that its claims are simple and cannot be evaded.

The British merchant service that Conrad joined was far from perfect, as this text has shown. Apprentices could count themselves lucky if they received any proper training.

Ships' masters were frequently either incompetent or incapable or both, through drink or age. Many owners were scandalously and indeed criminally miserly in the way that they treated ships' crews, and this affected everyone from master to lowliest ship's boy. Moreover, the life of a professional seaman was necessarily a harsh and dangerous one, it seemed: even the best ship might claim a victim from time to time, and ill-maintained, poorly designed or simply unlucky ships were regular killers. The great *Cutty Sark*, one of the last of the so-called clippers, and now preserved in all her beauty of line and form beside the Thames at Greenwich, had an unfortunate reputation for killing her crew. She was known as a 'wet' ship, meaning one whose decks were frequently swept by incoming waves: and woe betide the seaman who failed to jump or grasp for safety under such conditions!

However, the picture was not one of unrelieved gloom. There were good ships, with happy crews and respected masters – as it happened, like the outstanding Captain Woodget of the *Cutty Sark*, whose excellent safety record suggests that the ship's previously poor reputation was not the vagary of fate but the consequence of bad management. Life in the merchant service was not all rounding the Horn in the teeth of howling gales, constantly jumping for safety on deck, or hanging on desperately aloft whilst fighting recalcitrant canvas, and snatching the occasional half-hour's rest in sea-sodden clothing on a pitching bunk. Conrad had his share of hardship and struggle at sea, but there was beauty and delight as well: flying-fish passages, exuberant progress under the kindly and predictable trades with clear blue skies overhead and a horizon that beckoned. And when all was said and done, the true sailor reckoned on the hardships as part of the proper life at sea. He was not a fair-weather yachtsman, only venturing beyond the jetty on calm and sunny days, when the wind force was down to one or two. Even the monotonous food at sea, and the cramped living conditions of the foc's'l or crews' quarters elsewhere, were accepted as inevitable by most sailors, although they would complain loudly enough about particular injustices.

It was all part of the life, and they accepted it whole. Wooden ships required iron men, whose first duty was to the ship and not to themselves, as was brought out so strongly by Conrad in his first full-length story of life at sea, *The Nigger of the Narcissus*. 'Ships' lawyers', who quoted from Board of Trade regulations at every opportunity, were as unpopular for'ard as aft: the nineteenth-century sailing ship was no place for a shop steward. The professional seaman was stolid, stoical and fatalistic. He accepted the life at sea for what it was. When the voyage ended and he went ashore, he spent his pay and signed on for another voyage, as if unhappy to be on land. Ultimately every member of the crew depended on every other for his continued survival: and perhaps this influenced them in their attitude towards the lesser vicissitudes of fate.

To be an officer in the British merchant service was a unique experience, and one that left its mark on a man for life. He could be almost unbelievably bad at his job – in which case the sea would find him out in the end, but not before he had wrecked others' lives, if not his own – or superlatively good. It was up to him. Once he had obtained his certificates, and provided he could secure a position with them – which, as we have seen, was not the easiest of things to achieve – then a ship's officer could to a large extent set his own standard. And if that were true for the watch-keeping officer, it was even more so for the captain. He was accountable to no-one save the owner. He enjoyed or suffered the loneliness of command (so well explored in *The Secret Sharer*) and set his own standard. Conrad, as a master mariner, set himself a high one.

In choosing to go to sea and to master that difficult and exacting profession, the young refugee from Russian Poland was to gain a career, a language, a nationality and a name. Under that name, Joseph Conrad, and in that language, he was eventually to become an acclaimed and successful writer of enduring reputation. Indeed, he was to be described by the leading literary critic F. R. Leavis of Cambridge University as 'amongst the very greatest novelists in the language – or any language.'[20]

But it is to the memory and achievements of Captain Korzeniowski that this book is dedicated.

20. F. R. Leavis, *The Great Tradition*. Chatto and Windus, London, 1948.

Appendix
The merchant navy in Conrad's day

Ships' records

The Merchant Shipping Act (1854) required a ship's official documents to be preserved. These documents were the articles of agreement and the official log. Official logs were often very sparsely maintained, but could still be revealing. They were required, *inter alia*, to record all instances of births, marriages and deaths at sea, and any disciplinary measures taken. In addition, while at sea, ships maintained what was called a deck log. This was a watch-by-watch record of the progress of the ship. There was no legal requirement for this to be preserved, but some were. These sources are an invaluable record of the sailing ship in Conrad's day and beyond.

Survival of small sailing craft

In the 1850s, '60s, '70s and '80s many hundreds of little British, French, Italian, Spanish, Portuguese, German, Russian, Scandinavian, Dutch and American ships, very like Conrad's *Skimmer of the Sea*, plied the wide and narrow seas and got on with the world's work with quiet and inexpensive efficiency, costing little and polluting nothing – their modest earnings satisfying their owners and the life they offered satisfying their crews. Ships and crews lasted a long time usually, unless wrecked and lost together. Life expectancy of the average deep-sea and coastal seaman was perhaps not high, especially if he sailed in ships in trades to the west coast of South America or the west coast of Africa. In some ships' articles still in existence, the latter is expressly banned 'between Sierra Leone and Cape Frio'. This ban appears in the articles of the clipper *Sir Lancelot*, 885 tons, signed at South Shields on 28 September 1892. Well past her racing days, she was in the Indian trade then – jute from Calcutta to Rouen – and the articles also stated that fourteen hands all-told was a full crew. Captain Murdo McDonald of Stornaway in the Isle of Lewis must have been rather particular, for he also banned all Labrador and Greenland, though neither was a probable source of profitable cargo for the clipper.

Most ships' articles were more like those of the little *Nancy*, 213 tons, of Arklow, which banned nothing, even when she was setting out (also in 1892) on a simple passage from Runcorn to Riga, and 'thence to any port or ports no place excepted Voyage not to exceed 6 mos.' Those articles belied themselves, for it was impossible for the 213-ton *Nancy* to get far from Riga and back to Runcorn in the balance of six months left after her Riga voyage. The articles show that in fact she went straight to Riga and back. That world range was purely speculative, but minute square-riggers, ranging from a little over 200 tons to around 500, sailed out of Wales and Maryport, the Mersey, all Devon, Fleetwood and the other smaller ports of Britain and covered all the deep-sea trades until the turn of the twentieth century. Years after that, little ships of 450–600 tons remained in the Tasmania trade, which suited them; like the pint-size local clipper *Harriet McGregor*, built in Hobart, and Fenwick's 600-ton *Windward* of London, though every voyage meant a circumnavigation – out round Good Hope, back round the Horn. Similar small ships were on the non-stop trade between Britain and Brisbane, Adelaide or the Swan River, Western Australia, and many to New Zealand.

One factor which helped small ships like the *Skimmer of the Sea* to pay dividends was their ability to engage in local trading between charters, especially in Eastern waters. Once they had discharged their outward freight in good order, they could seek whatever employment of which the master (often also his own agent and usually part-owner) might hear. For example, the log of a little barque named *Ruth*, 468 tons, of Sunderland, for a voyage made from England between 5 April 1873 and 15 June 1874 (Christopher Minto, master) shows that after delivering her European cargo at Hong Kong as chartered (it was probably bunker-coal, for the use of steamships) she sailed at once in ballast for Saigon, where she loaded rice and cotton in the river. Her crew often did the stevedoring, and everything else. She took the Saigon cargo back to Hong Kong, discharged it, and loaded general cargo there for Saigon again, sailed there, delivered this and then took a full load of rice to Surabaya in Java. Here she picked up a sugar cargo for Falmouth. So she earned three nice freights 'on the side'.

It was not the development of steam which caused the decline of the smaller sailing ships, like the *Skimmer of the Sea*. It was the development of metal ships, first of iron, then of steel. For these leapt quickly to the 2,000-ton mark and beyond: obviously they served a different world in which the little fellow no longer belonged. Steam, meanwhile, was developing, and was eventually to put all sailing ships out of business; but this process took much longer than might have been expected in the 1870s.

Sail versus steam

The Suez Canal made powered competition infinitely more worthwhile, though Alfred Holt's Blue Funnel Line of Far East traders out of Liverpool had no need of the Egyptian ditch to make their efficient steamships profitable. They were operating effective, economical steamships of over 2,000 tons from Liverpool to China round Good Hope from 1866, three years before the canal was open. The SS *Agamemnon*, *Ajax* and *Hercules* of Holt's Ocean Steamship Company pioneered this service. Alfred Holt was the real genius of steam at sea, not the brilliant Brunel. What he, his partners and his very effective organisation did was to improve the performance of the ocean-going steamship 'to the point where speed and carrying capacity eventually produced a cost structure more economical than that of the sailing ship', as Professor Hyde put it in 1956.[21]

The *Agamemnon, Ajax* and *Hercules* of 1866 killed the deep-sea trade of the *Skimmer of the Sea*, the *Harriet McGregor* and all the rest of the sailing ships, small and (in time) large – or spelled their death notice, although it was a long time before many of them accepted it. Those most directly concerned hated to take note of trends they thought unnecessary and even – in a way – inhuman. After all, God provided His great gift of the ocean winds for the propulsion of ships, and it had taken foolish Man countless thousands of years to learn that much properly. Why then give it all up again for the bulking, sea-bruising, soul-destroying steamships?

The opening of the Suez Canal shortened the steamer's route to China by over 3,000 miles and permitted the early establishment of an efficient series of coaling stations at convenient wayside stops like Gibraltar, Suez, Aden, Colombo, Penang, Singapore, and Hong Kong – all then British, and most offering parcel cargoes in their own right. They also offered a large charter market for bunker-coal cargoes by sail (as did places elsewhere like Acapulco, Honolulu, Valparaiso, Callao and Panama, in due course), because the sailing ship could carry bunker-coal more cheaply than a steamer, for a long time. Thus the development of steam took away one type of cargo from sail, but gave another in exchange – for a while. In due course, more efficient steamships were to take over even in this field. But this explains why the *Palestine* was able to make her repeated attempts to carry coal to the Far East; there was a market, and she was a cheap carrier.

The loss of the *Palestine* (an all-too-frequent occurrence) may help to explain why owners (who could insure their ships) were happy enough to use their sailing ships in carrying coal for steamers; the masters and more thoughtful seamen were less appreciative.

It was much more difficult for the steamship to take over the really long-haul trades: to Australia and New Zealand, to Chile, to California. Here sail lasted to some extent at least into the first two decades of the twentieth century. The famous Laeisz Line of Germany carried Chilean nitrate to Europe by sail (in such outstanding vessels as the five-masted barque *Potosi*, and the five-masted ship *Preussen*) until the nitrate market itself was transformed by the development of artificial fertilisers – a consequence of wartime stoppage of imports.

The dangers of life at sea

Life at sea in sailing ships, large and small, was both hard and dangerous. Even on the best-run ship, members of the crew could be washed overboard or plucked from the rigging with frightening ease. A typical example comes from the official log of the 500-ton barque *Albert William* of Liverpool on a round voyage to Australia and South America. On the home leg, bound from Chile for Liverpool, and rounding the Horn in winter, a boy went

---

21. Francis E. Hyde, *Blue Funnel*. Liverpool University Press, Liverpool, 1956.

overboard. He was 'shifting the main royal halliards to windward', the better to support the mast, when he slipped and a sudden roll-down of the barque at that moment threw him over the side. Second mate Malcolm Malcolmsen 'took a line immediately and leapt after him: could not hold boy and rope: both lost: night, stormy, raining: threw over lifebuoy and beat ship back to search; saw nothing; could not launch boat which would also be lost.'

The second mate's listed gear included 'One quadrant, one chest, one epitome'. Boy Thos. Ambrose Oxley's includes '2 doz. paper collars, 2 shirt fronts, 1 slate, album, 2 handkerchiefs, 1 tie', and also a quadrant. He was only 15, but they were both professionals in a harsh life.

In the ship *Argus* of Glasgow, outward bound for Australia with general cargo on 2 July 1895, being in the Roaring Forties at the time and roaring along, third mate John Kelly lost his footing as the top of a sea clumped the foc's'l-head where he was working. The *Argus* lurched violently to leeward and hurled him overboard. Captain Laird saw what happened from the poop, threw a lifebuoy over, brought the ship to the wind, and saw the third mate reach the rescuing buoy. Out lee boat with volunteers! Everybody volunteered, at once – every man in the ship. Captain Laird sent his mate William Kelly – the third mate's cousin – with a crew of four able seamen (Duncan McLean, John Robertson, Findlay Macdonald, William Sharp) and Peter Lindsay, steward. The seas were very heavy, but these men had all been Scots fishermen and they could handle the boat. Captain Laird saw them pick up the third mate. He began to wear ship to run to them – so close! A vicious squall screamed down with hail. When it had blown over there was no boat, anywhere. Captain Laird beat upon the spot for two days and two nights with lookouts aloft, and the ship showing lights by night. Nothing was seen; nothing was ever seen.

Life expectancy for the crew of a crack clipper could be very poor. Clippers were built to be driven hard to make fast passages, and were dangerous, as the following quotations, chosen from the log of the beautiful *Thermopylae*, illustrate:

1869–70	Lost one A.B. from jib-boom: fell while furling jib: heavy gale: saw nothing: drowned. [His kit was two flannel shirts, two vests, two pairs of trousers, one jacket and one box. This pathetic outfit, which does not even include oilskins or sea-boots, unless he were wearing these when he was lost, may have been all this seaman possessed in the world; for the ship would have been, in all probability, his only home.]
1870–71	Lost the Bos'n overboard: died of heart failure while swimming strongly towards a lowered boat after being washed from the jib-boom. Known to have a bad heart: suddenly stopped swimming. Stayed at the place an hour but he did not surface again. His cap and a lifebuoy thrown to him were recovered. [Kit: sheepskin mat, tobacco cutters, 6 Crimean shirts, 1 reefing jacket, box candles, 6 silk handkerchiefs, 3 pr sleeping trousers, 1 navy cap, 1 prayer book, wages £5.5/- monthly; allotment £3.15/-. An extraordinary boatswain.]

1880–81	Mate and App. Augustus Collingridge drowned near Cape Horn. Washed overboard.
3.3.81–16.2.82	1 A.B. died at sea aged 39, 1 drowned do. [no details]
15.3.82–29.8.82	[London to London via Sydney] A.B. Robt. Scarlett died: Supt. satisfied there was no foul play.

By this time the crew, which had formerly been largely British, included many Scandi–navians, Finns, Germans, West Indians, an Icelander, an Australian or two, and a Russian. A Swede aged 22 was drowned on an 1887–88 voyage: how was not stated. The entry states, rather puzzlingly, that 'the ship did not sustain any loss or damage.' He, too, probably went overboard from the jib-boom – that mercilessly exposed long spar which gave a man no chance when a thrashing sail struck him off, or she threw her sharp nose under. Sail-maker William Goodchild was drowned on the following voyage, aged 53; and so many apprentices deserted from the clipper at Sydney that, well before 1890, there could have been a flourishing club of them from just that one ship.

During some of this time the *Thermopylae* was making real clipper passages from Sydney to the wool sales in London – one of 75 days and three of 79 are among those which Basil Lubbock lists as among her best between 1874 and 1890.[22] She appears to have been in Sydney once while Conrad was there, and so was the *Cutty Sark*, but he does not mention seeing either of them.

Most clippers seem to have been what sailing-ship seamen knew as 'wet' ships. In their expert opinion, such ships were likely to take far more sea over themselves than they should, and driving made them worse. Sharp ends got little lift from the assaulting sea, and some over-slip hulls could have stood more buoyancy. In many of these ships the helmsman took his life in his hands whenever the ship was running before a gale, and these were the most testing conditions for his skill. Despite his ability, sometimes the sea just reached up and swept wheel, wheel-box, helmsman and binnacle over the side with one blow. An entry in the official log of the clipper *Fiery Cross* on passage from the UK towards Hong Kong during her 1862–63 voyage refers to an AB 'washed from the wheel and drowned on 44–40 S. He was lashed with a 2½ inch line: much damage on the poop.'

During the previous voyage another AB was washed from for'ard. She rolled heavily and a sea leapt inboard and plucked him out, for the *Fiery Cross* of 689 tons was wet. Yet she survived a typhoon on a Yokohama voyage which took almost a year (including a call at New York) between 27 March 1871 and 3 March 1872. This struck the ship on 30.06 N, 131.30 E, according to her log, on 9 December 1871:

---

22. Captain Basil Lubbock, MC (1876–1944) quit Eton for the Klondyke gold rush in 1896 and later signed on the four-masted barque *Rosshire* as an ordinary seaman. He became an unequalled chronicler of the last days of sail.

Ship labouring and shipping fearful seas over fore and aft. Glass 28.90. Midnight main tops'l and mizzen stays'l blew away: put up a light sail in the mizzen rigging to keep her head to wind. At 4 a.m. Glass 28.50. At 8 the wind roaring like thunder and awful to look at the ship completely under water, all bulwarks gone from the break for the forecastle to the break of the poop. All livestock washed away. At noon same. Glass 28.55. Longboat stove ... expecting every moment the masts to go.

There it is in the raw. Typhoon! The most dreaded storm in the world. No Conrad here, this plain and ungrammatical chronicler, fearful for his ship with dreadful cause: this is the plain seaman James Middleton, aged 46, a man who had spent his life from the age of 13 in hard ships. He had had no time to master grammar, nor to feel the loss. The next entry in his official log that voyage shows his little *Fiery Cross* in New York. She was a small ship, but her draft when laden is often recorded as the best part of 19 feet – very likely she was overloaded. She must have been a strong, good little ship, well handled by a succession of tough masters.

Discipline at sea

A fascinating insight into how masters maintained, or sometimes failed to maintain, discipline in their ships can be discovered from the official logs. The log of the famous clipper *Lightning* when she was commanded by Anthony Enright gives the bare facts from which one can infer some tempestuous voyages, for Captain Enright was clearly a harsh master and a hard driver, a man who had made a reputation for making fast passages in other ships, and intended to add to it in the *Lightning*.

In 1855, off the Horn en route for Australia with emigrants, Captain Enright disrated his fourth mate for wasting fresh water; he also disrated a quartermaster for bad helmsmanship. Captain Enright's standards were high. A bad helmsman might add an hour to the voyage. The ship's butcher fetched up in irons for the heinous crime of wasting fresh meat (doubtless from a beast slain on board, for these clipper passenger ships carried a small stockyard and quite a fowl-run). The butcher's offence must have been regarded as unusually serious, as the log says he was ironed in the maintop for several days, a few hours at a time, the 'few' not specified. This hazardous proceeding so irked his shipmates that (the log records) one of them – the boatswain no less, named as Charles Pearson – ran up to the top, took off the irons and flung them in the sea. Boatswain Pearson was arrested for this manifest act of defiance and charged with mutiny. On reflection, Captain Enright must have thought that the punishment was perhaps dangerous, for the tops were windy, exposed, extremely cold, and very lively. No case was heard against the boatswain.

The *Lightning* had a large crew including four officers as well as a bos'n, bos'n's mate and second bos'n, six apprentices and droves of tough Liverpool-Irish lads before the mast – those same hard, competent but sometimes hot-headed seamen who had lapped up the Irish Sea with their mother's milk, and had kept the leaking migrant-carriers going in the Western Ocean, summer and winter. These were the guts of Liverpool's sea strength, just as so many of their land-bound countrymen were the core of great fighting regiments in the British Army. Any clipper was a tough job for an able seaman: there was no glamour in such ships for him. On those 'Gold Rush' runs they saw no gold and the only 'rush' they knew was from their own grim, hard-worked ship, as soon as her anchor was down and sails furled, to the prison-hulk hard-by. Here their hard-driving captain had them imprisoned on trumped-up charges of indiscipline, to prevent them from running for the diggings; they would be released when the ship was ready to sail.

More irons are in use on the following voyage, in 1856. The state of discipline must have been poor, for she has not gone far before all hands are refusing to do anything not directly concerned with the safety, sailing or cleanliness of the ship (according to the official log). In the doldrums – that trying area where the best tempers may fray – a petulant log-note observes that the starboard watch 'were 1 hr 30 min setting the fore topmast studding-sail', which indicates at least a degree of bloody-mindedness, for the job should have taken about ten minutes. A day or two later, the whole starboard watch is collectively logged for 'treating Mr Black 2nd Mate with disrespect such as singing at their work mornings holystoning the poop.' They are kept at work an extra hour (still singing?), whereat the port watch stayed in their forecastle instead of relieving them. This is a depressing account, the deep-seated roots of future industrial trouble – boss against men, men against boss, mostly about nothing except perhaps here the frustration of the doldrums, with a large number of passengers to look on. By 12 October the log records open warfare. The second mate

> shook John Davies more than he pleased, and he struck at him. A fight ensued ... Mark Morgan A.B. deliberately struck the Captain without cause. I, imagining a general combat being about to begin fetched two cutlasses one I gave to Mr McDonald the other I used myself by striking Wm. Paulsen with the flat of it, who was fighting with Mr Black.

And so order was restored for the time being. The next day, able seaman Charles Napier,

> rigging out the main top-mast stud'g. sail boom too slowly told the mate 'not to be in a bloody hurry'. Called to the deck. Being impudent I was obliged to strike him, as did the 2nd Mate, and made him go to work.

Two of them, with the flats of cutlasses?

A week or two later, the log is recording the story of a seaman seen breaking into the saloon (from which some hard liquor had been disappearing). 'I rope's-ended him heartily,' writes the second mate, 'and put him in irons too.' The rope's-ended, handcuffed AB denied that he had touched any liquor in the saloon (and discipline must indeed have been slack if he could do such a thing). The irons were removed but he said then he was so stiff from the beating he couldn't do his work. He was ironed again.

The ship reached Australia after making an indifferent passage (despite, or perhaps because of, Captain Enright's slave-driving efforts). There some crewmen deserted and were expensively replaced; and she returned to England without further record of mutiny or fighting. She had a good passage this time.

By August 1857 (at the time of Conrad's birth), the *Lightning* was outward bound from England for Calcutta with troops to help quell the Indian Mutiny. Anthony Enright, having driven her well for several years, went ashore at Gravesend and was succeeded by Edward Byrne. The crew nationalities by this time were very mixed, but the majority was still British. An AB fell from aloft: slipping off a topgallant yard when struck by a sudden ballooning back of the bunt of the sail, he hit the crosstrees on the way down and bounced overboard; it was not customary to have an emergency boat ready, possibly because the sea could so easily take it away, and so he was lost. At Calcutta the deck crew refused duty; 33 of them, says the log, were jailed for a month forthwith. When they returned aboard there was more trouble, perhaps naturally.

The *Lightning*'s Indian interlude lasted from 16 August 1857 to November 1858 – a long time for the one voyage. Queen Victoria paid a visit to one of the big American-built clippers at Portsmouth, the *James Baines*, before the ship sailed, and is reported to have declared that she 'was not aware that so splendid a merchant ship belonged to her dominions', but neither the Queen nor her court was well informed on such matters. Clippers and all such ships did not often come to the Royal notice. The *Champion of the Seas* was also put to troop-carrying, and the three big racers did their best. The *James Baines* and the *Champion* each took 101 days from Portsmouth to the mouth of the Hooghli, but the *Lightning*, sailing later, was only 87 days. She was reported to have made a better passage than all other ships in that great army-moving fleet, even those fitted with power.

But this was a once-only charter. For the *James Baines* it was her last, as she was destroyed by fire while discharging her Indian cargo in Liverpool. The *Lightning* was back in the Australian trade in 1859, and lasted ten more years: she did not again record the sort of near-mutinous situation Captain Enright had had to contend with.

Passengers under sail

Conrad sailed in several sailing ships which carried, or had carried, passengers. The *Torrens* was one, and the *Duke of Sutherland* another; but even the little *Skimmer of the Sea* had been a passenger-carrier in her time. In the 1870s and '80s sailing ships still brought many passengers to Australia, especially large organised parties of migrants, for primitive accommodation fitted temporarily in the hold sufficed for them, and they were profitable enough as cargo. The hold was always subdivided into three compartments – aft for single women, midships for married couples and families and for'ard for the single men, with a medical officer to look after them all.

Such passengers made a lively ship. They provided their own amusements, concerts, theatre and the rest; and any handy or enterprising seaman could both help them and profit from them (in a small way) by cobbling shoes, running a bit of a rough-and-ready laundry when rain permitted, trimming the men's hair, selling a bit of fancy-work such as decorated sea-bags, sea-chest handles, bell-ropes and the like, and even bringing along some popular fiction and running a small library at a penny a book each loan. A shipboard paper was always produced, and a good master kept the iron hand well hidden in his velvet glove while he ruled with effective and firm benevolence.

Discipline at sea was necessary, for controlling passengers (and crew) at sea could be difficult. In Geelong, according to a Police Court case reported in the Melbourne *Argus* (of 8 July 1852), five able seamen of the ship *Sir Robert Sale* were charged with breaches of discipline on the passage out. It transpired that among other things, 'they wouldn't let the girls alone' – but the evidence showed very clearly that 'some of the damsels would not leave their favourite tars alone either.' Despite this, the Bench showed that discipline must come before love. The five had also been insolent to the master, and they went to jail.

The evolution of the merchant navy

Steam replaced sail, as it was bound to do, but took a long time to do so. Curiously enough the Royal Navy, that supposedly most conservative and crusty of institutions, was quick to make the change; the merchant navy was much slower. In the end, it all came down to the harsh facts of economics. Once steam was cheaper than sail, sail was doomed. However, there was no cutoff point when steam became indisputably cheaper, for all routes and all cargoes; and the merchant sailing ship continued to develop and improve even though steam had already signalled its eventual extinction.

The old-established and very well-respected Laeisz shipping line of Hamburg was still building full-rigged sailing ships in the twentieth century, and was to persist in sail, and to make a profit in doing so, long after almost all its contemporaries had given up what seemed a hopeless struggle with the force of destiny, and moved into steam.

Why were the Laeisz ships successful for so long? They were well built, properly fitted and maintained, well manned and officered, and designed and fitted to do precisely what they were best at: long deep-sea passages from Germany to Chile and Peru around the Horn and back, ferrying nitrates from the South American west-coast desert-ports to satisfy the insatiable demands of both agricultural and industrial Germany. Nitrates came from guano, and guano was the excrement left by the millions of seabirds who used the coast of Chile as a thousand-league latrine. Guano was gold. Ashore as afloat, the Laeisz company thought ahead, keeping its own agents and ensuring that cargoes were ready for loading when needed.

The crews of the Laeisz ships were chosen with care – in clear contrast to the British merchant navy in the time of Captain Konrad Korzeniowski, when no such solicitude was exercised – and good sailors and tradesmen were paid a bounty to re-enlist. Officers were selected carefully, given the right experience at the right time, and groomed, if they had the potential, for eventual high command. Ferdinand Laeisz promoted on merit and merit alone, and his fleet had no commodore; a captain who showed the ability could command any ship in the fleet.

The Laeisz Line had also benefited from the thoroughly professional approach of the German merchant navy as a whole, which included the collection and collation of complete meteorological records for all routes sailed. No wonder Alan Villiers called the relevant chapter of his book on the development of the sailing ship 'The thorough Germans'.[23]

An outstanding example of a Laeisz ship's officer was Captain Robert Miethe, one of the greatest sailing-ship sailors who ever lived. Born in 1877 in Holstein, Germany, he went to sea as a boy of 14 and shipped deep sea in 1893 from Hamburg. By the beginning of 1900 he had been eight years at sea and was 22 years old. It was time to move abaft the mast. Young Miethe took his mate's certificate – a very searching examination in the German merchant service – at his first sitting, and worked his way up to mate of the *Preussen* – a giant five-masted full-rigged ship, the largest ever built of its kind, and the pride of her company. She was eventually lost in the Channel in 1910, run down by a steamer who could not estimate her speed. Many sailing ships were lost in such collisions – the fate of the *Ferndale* in Conrad's *Chance*.

Robert Miethe served as chief officer of the *Preussen*, and went on to command the *Potosi*, a giant five-masted barque, again designed for the nitrate trade, in which she rounded the Horn many times. The *Potosi* was one of the finest sailing ships ever built and achieved *consistently* remarkable performances under sail alone. She made use of every relevant development that was available (including powered winches at the main hatches) and her enormous spread of canvas was able to be handled in (comparative) safety by a relatively small crew. This was at least in part due to the sensible use by the Germans of British innovations, some of them the pioneering work of Captain J. C. B. 'Bracewinch' Jarvis, which were not generally adopted in British ships.

Captain Jarvis was a great innovator, one of those men who refused to accept the prejudice (always held by generation after generation of old seamen each in their own era) that the sea-going sailing ship was incapable of further improvement. His real ambition, as he told Alan Villiers many years later, was to design and sail a new type of sailing ship in which the sails were controlled from below, as on a Chinese junk, and the crew was not washed overboard from the ship's decks whilst handling those sails, because the vessel had been designed to protect them at their work (more seamen were lost by being washed from the decks of the old square-rigger than by falling from the rigging). Simplified masts and rigging would allow the vessel to lie close to the wind, making better to windward; and other sensible and pragmatic changes would be made. Such a ship never sailed, for Jarvis's ideas were not supported.

Neither *Preussen* nor *Potosi*, massive ships as they were, was an easy sailer; and perhaps Captain Miethe's favourite command was the *Pitlochry*, for she was one of those rather rare big square-riggers which were responsive to the lightest whisper of the wind, the least touch of the helm. (Old seamen who knew her agreed that the *Thermopylae* was another such joy to sail, but not the *Cutty Sark*, which did not quite match that natural perfection.)

23. Alan Villiers, *The War with Cape Horn* (Hodder and Stoughton, London, 1971), chapter 12.

Robert Miethe told Alan Villiers with reminiscent pride – in the ship, not in himself – of an occasion in 1910 when he beat the *Pitlochry* up the length of the English Channel and lower North Sea during a week of glorious summer. Once he stood in toward the English side until he was a ship's length off the end of Brighton pier, in perfect conditions. The long pier was full of summer visitors. Bands played. Gay throngs were ready for a spectacle. Miethe gave them a memorable one, for he spun the great four-masted barque in her own length right before their eyes, giving them such a demonstration of Cape Horn ship-handling as few had seen before and none would ever see again. On she came at first with the shoaling green Channel water turned to froth at the lovely bow, this great German ship with the Scots name, silent except for the slight lisp of her own way and the whisper of the afternoon wind. Still she sailed onward, bounding at the rate of many knots.

Suddenly an order! Up flew the mainsail and crojack, bunted up in their gear almost like blinds. Spanker to wind'ard, jibs flapping with their restraining sheets let go, into the wind came the beautiful ship, sweeping her bowsprit end into the wind's eye off the end of the pier. Sails thrashed, blocks rattled, as the lines sang through them.

Mains'l haul!

Around came main and mizzen yards, as if by clockwork. Around swung the ship, her head pushed swiftly by the backed sails on the fore. Now all sail on main and mizzen filled: the ship stood a moment, then began to gather way.

Let go and haul!

Around came the headyards, lee braces let go and weather braces manned, foretack and sheet tended, jib and stays'l sheets shifted over. The great ship leaned again to the wind. Down came main and crojack tacks and sheets. Under all sail again, off sprang the thoroughbred, biting to wind'ard, now on the tack out to sea.

The huge crowd cheered spontaneously to see such perfection so perfectly handled, though indeed unaware of that. But the magnificent spectacle stirred them all. 'A man may know an occasion like that only once in a lifetime,' said the old man.

Glossary

Aback – Square sails are aback when the wind is on the wrong side, i.e. blowing them into rather than away from the mast. To go aback can be dangerous for a sailing ship in strong winds as her masts and rigging are designed to withstand the greatest wind pressure from the sides and the stern.

Abaft – Towards the stern.

Able seaman, AB – Experienced seaman, paid more than an ordinary seaman (OS). AB stands for able-bodied.

Afterguard – The ship's officers, the master and mates, who live aft.

Auxiliary – A sailing vessel which also has an engine.

Barque – A vessel with three or more masts, fore-and-aft rigged on the aftmost mast only; otherwise square-rigged.

Barquentine – A vessel with three or more masts, square-rigged on the foremast only and fore-and-aft rigged on the other masts.

Battened down – A vessel has been battened down when her hatches have been sealed with canvas and battens by the ship's carpenter and she is ready to go to sea.

Beam – The widest part of a vessel; the width of the vessel.

Beam-ends – A vessel is 'on her beam-ends' when she lies horizontal or practically horizontal in the sea and her deck is practically vertical.

Beat, to – To work a sailing vessel to windward by making a series of tacks, thus progressing against the direction of the wind.

Binnacle – A case or box to house the compass, fitted with a lamp for night use.

Boat – A ship's boat is a small vessel, used for such tasks as communication between ship and shore.

Boatswain, Bos'n – A ship's officer in charge of mustering the crew and maintaining the rigging.

Boom – A long spar used to extend or 'boom out' the foot of a sail.

Braces – Lines used on a square-rigged vessel to rotate the yards around the mast, to allow the ship to sail at different angles to the wind.

Brig – A two-masted square-rigged vessel.

Brigantine – A two-masted vessel, square-rigged on the foremast only.

Bulwarks – A barrier between seaman and sea, around the main deck

Buntline – A rope attached to the foot-rope of a sail to aid in furling it.

Caulk – To caulk a vessel is to render watertight the seams between her planks, using oakum, a preparation of tarred fibres.

Clew – The lower corner of a square sail.

Clipper – An inexact term for a fast sailing-ship, with sharp lines and reduced cargo-carrying capacity, designed and sailed for speed. *The Cutty Sark*, *Thermopylae* and *Fiery Cross* were all classic clippers; there were many more.

Close to the wind – To sail close to the wind, or close-hauled, is to sail as near as possible against the direction of the wind.

Club-haul – A method of tacking a vessel in a crisis, involving dropping the anchor and then cutting or slipping the anchor cable.

Counter – The part of a ship from the waterline to the angle of the stern. Ships' boats would often hold off below her counter.

Course – The point of the compass on which the ship sails. Also the lower sails, such as the foresail and mainsail.

Crew – The crew of a sailing ship would usually consist of the master and his mates; the bos'n, carpenter and sail-maker; the cook and steward; and the seamen. Seamen were divided into able seamen, ordinary seamen and boys. A passenger ship might carry extra stewards and perhaps a doctor.

Crojack – The first square sail above the deck on the mizzen.

Crosstrees – Horizontal timbers projecting from the mast, to support the shrouds (the rigging which is stretched from the mast to the sides of the vessel).

Cutter – A ship's boat or other small vessel, generally single-masted and fore-and-aft rigged.

Cutwater – The foremost part of a vessel's prow.

Disrate – To reduce a member of the ship's crew in rank as a punishment (this would result in reduced pay)

Doldrums – An area of the oceans near the equator where the trade winds are not found and sailing ships often make very slow progress.

Donkey engine – An engine carried on a vessel to ship or discharge the cargo or raise the anchor (the engine is thus metaphorically in place of a donkey). As both the sailing ship and internal combustion engines evolved, donkey engines came into use on sailing ships. This meant that fewer crew needed to be carried and costs were lower.

Easting, run down – Easting means the distance sailed eastward. A ship was said to 'run her easting down' as she sailed the long eastward leg from the Cape of Good Hope to Australia, or from Australia to Cape Horn.

Eight bells – Working time on a ship is traditionally divided into six watches of four hours. The ship's bell is rung to signal the passage of each half-hour. Eight bells means that four hours is complete and the watch changes.

Fore-and-aft – The opposite of square-rigged: sails which are set along the line of the keel rather than at right angles to it, and not set to yards.

Forecastle, Foc's'l – Accommodation for the crew in the bows of a ship, later replaced by a steel deck-house.

Full-and-by – A vessel is sailing full-and-by when she is sailing close-hauled, but with some margin for error, to avoid being taken aback.

Full-rigged ship – A vessel with three or more masts, all square-rigged.

Gaff – A spar to which is tied the head of a fore-and-aft sail.

Half-deck – The aft section of a vessel's main deck, the territory of the second mate, apprentices, bos'n and other secondary officers.

Halliard, Halyard – a line used for raising and lowering the sails.

Heads – The latrine on board ship was known as the heads, from its traditional position on a structure projecting from the bows.

Holystoning – Scrubbing the decks using a type of sandstone called a holystone, or with a mixture of sand, water and small stones.

Horse latitudes – An area of the oceans with slight or fickle wind; like the doldrums but between 30 and 35 degrees north or south.

Jib-boom – A spar projecting from the bowsprit.

Kedge – A kedge anchor is a supplementary anchor; it may be used to haul a ship by continually shifting the anchor ahead and warping the vessel up to it.

Knot – The speed of a ship (or of the wind), in nautical miles per hour.

Lead-line – A line attached to the upper part of the sounding-lead, used for making soundings in shoal water: in other words, finding out the sea's depth below the ship. Depth is measured in fathoms of six feet.

Lee, Leeward – The lee side of the ship is opposite the windward or weather side. Where the wind is going to, rather than coming from.

Lee shore – A shore onto which the wind is driving, highly dangerous for a sailing-ship with no independent source of power.

Lighter – A powerless vessel used for transporting cargo, similar to a barge.

Limejuicer – A British sailing ship, so named because limejuice was issued as a preventative to scurvy.

Log – The ship's official log is a formal record of the ship's passage, maintained by her master. It is also a mechanical device towed from the stern and used for measuring speed.

Masts – A traditional full-rigged ship (also known simply as a ship) has three masts, fore, main and mizzen. The foremast is towards the bow of the ship and the mizzenmast or mizzen is towards the stern. Ships may have more than three masts, in which case the rearmost mast may be called the jigger, spanker or driver.

Mizzen royal – Usually the uppermost sail on the mizzen.

Pin-rail – A rail fitted to accept belaying-pins, around which the running rigging is made fast (or belayed).

Poop – A raised deck running from mizzen to stern, containing accommodation underneath for the ship's officers (the afterguard).

Port – Left-hand side of the vessel facing forward.

Ratline – A small horizontal rope between the shrouds, forming a rope ladder for climbing aloft.

Reef – To reef a sail is to reduce its area when the weather requires this. Sails can be single-, double- or triple-reefed.

Sails – The standard sails for the main mast of a full-rigged ship, working from the deck up, would be as follows:
- Mainsail (or main course)
- Main topsail
- Main topgallant
- Main royal
- Main skysail

Topsails and topgallant sails may be divided into lower and upper topsails and topgallants.

Schooner – a vessel with two or more masts, all rigged fore-and-aft.

Shanghai – To shanghai a crew is to enlist them by illegal or irregular means, as once practised in the port of Shanghai.

Sheet – A line attached to the lower corner (clew) of a sail, used to haul the corner of the sail down towards the tip of the yard below, or towards the deck. On a square-rigged sail the sheet alone does not control the angle of the sail (as it does for a fore-and-aft rig): that function is also performed by braces and tacks.

Ship – Strictly, only a full-rigged ship is a ship.

Spanker – A gaff-rigged fore-and-aft sail set on the aftmost mast.

Spar – A pole of wood or metal serving as a mast, yard, boom, etc.

Square-rigged – A sail plan in which the spars (yards) which support the sails are at right angles to the keel of the vessel, as opposed to a fore-and-aft rig.

Starboard – Right-hand side of the ship facing forward.

Stay – Fixed rigging to support a mast.

Stem – The bow or front of a ship.

Sternway – To make sternway is to go backwards rather than forwards.

Studding sail, Stuns'l – A sail used to increase the sail area of a square-rigged vessel in light winds. It is hoisted alongside a square sail on an extension of its yard.

Tack – (a) To tack is to change direction by pointing the bow into and across the wind, thus changing the side exposed to the wind. (b) A tack denotes the course that a vessel is sailing relative to the wind: if the wind is blowing from the starboard side she is on starboard tack; if the wind is blowing from the port side she is on port tack. (c) The tack of a square-rigged sail is a line attached to its lower corner (or clew).

Ticket – A ship's officer's certificate of competency is traditionally referred to as a 'ticket.' In the British merchant navy, an officer needs to obtain his second mate's, mate's and master's ticket, if he is to command a ship, whether in sail or steam. He may go on to take his 'ticket' as 'extra master', but this is not necessary for command. A ship may sign on an 'uncertificated' second mate under some circumstances, but the mate and master must have their certificates or tickets. When Conrad took command of the Otago, the acting master who had brought her to port on the death at sea of the ship's captain had no certificate as a master mariner and therefore could not be confirmed in command.

Topgallant, T'gallant – The sail above the topsail.

Topsail, Tops'l – The second sail on the mast, counting from the deck upwards.

Tops'l schooner – A schooner carrying some square sails, usually on the foremast alone.

Trade winds – The prevailing winds in the tropics and subtropics, blowing from the high-pressure area in the horse latitudes towards the low-pressure area around the equator. The trade winds blow predominantly from the northeast in the northern hemisphere and from the southeast in the southern hemisphere.

Tramp – A tramp ship carries any cargo anywhere and is only bound for one voyage at a time.

Trim – Cargo, ballast and sails may all be trimmed. The vessel's trim refers to how the cargo is stowed in order to ensure stability. Sails are trimmed to adjust their angle to the wind.

Truck – A wooden cap fitted at the head of a mast or flagstaff.

Waist – The middle of the ship.

Washboard – A plank fastened to and projecting above the side of the vessel, or around a cabin door etc., to keep out the spray and the sea.

Watches – Most sailing-ship crews were divided into two watches, one headed by the mate and the other by the second mate. The day was divided into six watches of four hours: 8 to 12, 12 to 4, and 4 to 8, twice, with the watch from 4 to 8 pm generally subdivided into two 'dog-watches' of two hours each, which served to break up the routine of having the same watch period (e.g. 8 am to noon) every day. On modern ships a three-watch system is more usual. The master does not stand a watch, but takes command when he pleases. It would be exceptional for the master not to be in command when the ship is in heavy weather, or carrying out complex manoeuvres, or entering or leaving port.

Wear ship – To bring a vessel onto the other tack by turning away from the wind and swinging her round by means of the wind blowing from behind into the sails (coming before the wind). Generally a safer manoeuvre than tacking, in a square-rigger.

Weather – The weather side of a vessel is the windward side, the side from which the wind and weather are coming. Hence weather bow, weather brace, weather clew, etc. The opposite is the lee or leeward side.

Windjammer – Originally, a term of abuse for a heavy and slow-to-respond sailing ship. Later, any large sailing vessel.

Yacht – A vessel sailed or steamed for pleasure, usually fore-and-aft rigged.

Yard – A horizontal spar to which the top edge of a square sail is fastened.

Yardarm – Either end of a yard.

Peter Villiers

Peter Villiers has written books on policing, leadership, ethics and human rights, but this is his first biography. He served in the merchant navy between school and university and later completed an extended short-service commission in the Royal Armoured Corps, soldiering in Northern Ireland, Cyprus and Hong Kong before becoming a police adviser and consultant who discovered his own interest in writing through creating leadership exercises. The result was his first book, *Twenty Workshops for Developing Leadership*, and the habit of writing, once begun, was hard to give up.

Peter accompanied his father on many ventures abroad, including ship-related visits to Stockholm, the Åland Islands, and both eastern and western seaboards of South America when Alan Villiers was researching the voyage of the *Beagle*. Later they were to visit the retired sea captain Robert Miethe, who had rounded the Horn many times under sail before embracing a life ashore in Chile. Peter Villiers shares his father's love of the sea and his admiration for Joseph Conrad.

Mark Myers, RSMA, F/ASMA

Mark Myers is a Californian-born marine artist, sailor and historian who developed a passion for sailing ships and seafaring in his early youth. These interests were fostered by the staff at the San Francisco Maritime Museum and a study of history at university, and through an acquaintance with Alan Villiers he was able to gain working experience on board a number of traditional sailing vessels. Self-taught as an artist, he held his first one-man exhibition in San Francisco in 1967. After a few more years in sail and further American exhibitions, he settled in England in 1971 to marry and concentrate on his research and painting. He was elected a member of the Royal Society of Marine Artists in 1975, becoming the Society's President from 1993 to 1998. He is also a charter member and Fellow of the American Society of Marine Artists. His work can be found in many public and private collections around the world and has been widely published in the form of book and magazine illustrations and fine art prints.

Index

CRUISE OF THE CONRAD

*A Journal of a Voyage round the World,
undertaken and carried out in the Ship
JOSEPH CONRAD, 212 Tons, in the Years
1934, 1935, and 1936 by way of Good Hope,
the South Seas, the East Indies, and Cape Horn*

ALAN VILLIERS

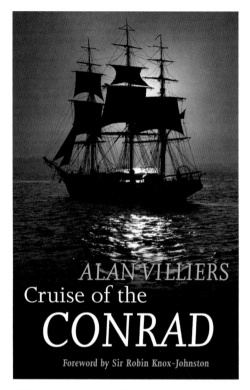

In 1934 the Australian sailor and writer Alan
Villiers set out to fulfil his life's ambition – to
obtain, equip and sail a full-rigged ship around
the world, and enthuse others with his own
love of sail before the opportunity was lost
for ever. He was successful. His record of that
extraordinary journey, more odyssey than
voyage, was first published in 1937. In this new
edition, complete with a short biography of Alan Villiers and richly illustrated with his
own photographs, it will inspire a new generation of sailors and sea-enthusiasts.

No other book like this will ever be written
> *The Sunday Times*

**'I will do no stunts and will have no ballyhoo,' Alan Villiers said when he bought
the ship in Copenhagen. And he kept to that from beginning to end of the voyage
recorded in this book. The voyage of the *Joseph Conrad* is the truthful story of a
great voyage, packed with adventure and the joy of a fine ship in full sail.**
> *from the first edition*

*Withe a foreword by Sir Robin Knox-Johnston
Illustrated with photographs*

UK   ISBN 0-9547062-8-5   £12.95 + p&p
USA   ISBN 1-57409-241-3 $17.95 + p&p

THE WAPPING GROUP OF ARTISTS

Sixty years of painting by the Thames

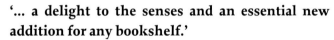

For sixty years, members of the Wapping Group have met to paint by the River Thames en plein air. Outdoors and undaunted in all weathers, come rain or shine, they have set up their easels from the broad tideways of the estuary to the willow-fringed backwaters up-river – taking in the whole of riverside London in between.

With 200 illustrations, the story of the group since 1946, a meditation on the pleasures and pains of painting outdoors, and personal accounts by all the current members, this book captures the essence of the Wapping Group, "the last proper artists' society left in England".

'... a delight to the senses and an essential new addition for any bookshelf.'
> *E14 Magazine*

'Sixty years after it was created, the Wapping Group is still flourishing and has won itself a secure niche in the artistic life of the capital ...'
> *Classic Boat*

UK   ISBN 0-9547062-5-0   £19.95 + p&p
USA   ISBN 1-57409-218-9 $29.95 + p&p

ROUGH PASSAGE
COMMANDER R. D. GRAHAM

In 1934 Commander R. D. Graham sailed alone in his 30-foot yacht *Emanuel* from England to Newfoundland, cruised on the coast of Labrador, fell ill, sailed to Bermuda in November ('twenty-three days of uninterrupted misery'), wintered there, and finally brought his little vessel back across the Atlantic to her old moorings in Poole Harbour.

Also included is *The Adventure of the Faeroe Islands*, an account of *Emanuel*'s 1929 voyage by R. D. Graham's daughter Helen (later Helen Tew). But when it came to the transatlantic crossing, Commander Graham left his mate of many years behind. 'It seemed a particularly treacherous proceeding sailing off without her,' he wrote, and his daughter never forgave him until she too had crossed the Atlantic at the age of 88 – as described in her own book, *Transatlantic At Last*.

This new edition of the seafaring classic is brought up to date by Robert Holden's account of the recent restoration of *Emanuel*, allowing R. D. Graham's 'little yacht' to take her rightful place as part of Britain's maritime heritage.

This is a must-read for anyone with the slightest interest in the sea, or in human nature.

Illustrated with photographs

'One of the most remarkable small-boat adventures of this or any other time
   Arthur Ransome

One of the 'great cruising accounts' listed in Peter Spectre's *A Mariner's Miscellany*

UK   ISBN 0-9547062-4-2   £9.95 + p&p
USA   ISBN 1-57409-212-X $14.95 + p&p